CURRICULUM:
PRODUCT OR PRAXIS?

Deakin Studies in Education Series

General Editors: Professor Rob Walker and Dr Stephen Kemmis,
Deakin University, Victoria, Australia

Deakin Studies in Education Series: 1

CURRICULUM: PRODUCT OR PRAXIS?

Shirley Grundy

 The Falmer Press

(A member of the Taylor & Francis Group)
London, New York and Philadelphia

UK   The Falmer Press, Falmer House, Barcombe, Lewes, East Sussex, BN8 5DL

USA   The Falmer Press, Taylor & Francis Inc., 242 Cherry Street, Philadelphia, PA 19106–1906

First published 1987

Library of Congress Cataloging-in-Publication Data

Grundy, Shirley.
   Curriculum: product or praxis.

   (Deakin studies in education series; 1)
   Bibliography: p.
   Includes index.
   1. Curriculum planning.   2. Teacher participation in curriculum planning.   3. Curriculum planning—Philosophy.
I. Title   II. Series.
LB2806.15.G78   1987   375'.001   87–13650
ISBN 1–85000–204–5
ISBN 1–85000–205–3 (pbk.)

Printed & bound in Great Britain by
Redwood Burn Limited, Trowbridge, Wiltshire

Contents

General Editors' Introduction

The Deakin Studies in Education Series aims to present a broad critical perspective across a range of interrelated fields in education. The intention is to develop what might be called a 'critical educational science': critical work in the philosophy of education, curriculum, educational and public administration, language education, and educational action research and clinical supervision. The series strives to present the writings of a rising generation of scholars and researchers in education.

A number of researchers based at Deakin University have been closely associated with the development of the critical perspective across these fields. For such reasons, people in the field have sometimes spoken of a 'Deakin perspective'. We do share some common views from which we hope to contribute to contemporary debates about the future development of educational enquiry; at the same time, our disagreements seem as fruitful for us as our agreements.

The Deakin Studies in Education Series provides an opportunity for extending this debate about the nature and future development of education and educational enquiry. It will include the writings of a variety of educational researchers around the world who, like ourselves, are interested in exploring the power and limitations of the critical perspective in the analysis of educational theory, policy and practice.

The central themes of the series will not be dictated by the alleged boundaries between 'foundational' disciplines in education, nor by an unexamined division of the tasks of education and educational research between 'practitioners' and 'theorists', or between 'practitioners', and 'policy-makers'. On the contrary, one of the tasks of the series is to demonstrate, through careful research and scholarship across a range of fields of practical, political ad theoretical endeavour, just how outmoded, unproductive, and ultimately destructive these divisions are both for education and for educational research. Put positively, the central themes and questions to be addressed in the series include:

> the unity of educational theory and practice — expressed, for example, in the work of educational practitioners who research their practice as a basis for improving it, and in the notion of collaborative, participatory educational research, for example, in educational action research;
> the historical formation, social construction and continual reconstruction of education and educational institutions and reforms through processes of contestation and institutionalization — expressed, for example, in the work of critical researchers into the curriculum and educational reform; and
> the possibilities of education for emancipation and active and productive participation in a democratic society — expressed, for example, in the development of critical pedagogy and the development of communitarian perspectives in the organization of education.

These are enduring themes, touching upon some of the central questions confronting our contemporary culture and, some would say, upon the central pathologies of contemporary society. They are all too easily neglected or obscured in the narrow and fragmented views of education and educational research characteristic of our times. Yet education is one of the key resources in what Raymond Williams once described as our societies' 'journey of hope' — the journey towards a better, more just, more rational and more rewarding society. Education has always aimed to nurture, represent, vivify and extend the values and modes of life which promise to make the best in our culture better. Finding out how this can be done, interpreting our progress, and appraising and reappraising the quality of our efforts at educational improvement are the tasks of critical educational research. They are the tasks of this series.

Stephen Kemmis and Rob Walker
April 1987

Acknowledgments

I would like to express my gratitude to a number of people for the parts they have played in bringing this work to fruition.

I owe a substantial intellectual debt to Stephen Kemmis of Deakin University who not only introduced me to some of the work which is fundamental to this book, but also opened doors on so many ideas which have subsequently proved to have been worth pursuing.

My thanks also to many colleagues at Murdoch University who nurtured my intellectual development while I was amongst them, especially Jane Kenway and David Tripp with whom so many of these ideas have been argued through.

I am also grateful to the students in my course, 'Foundations of Curriculum Theory and Development' at the University of New England, who grappled with and affirmed many of the ideas expressed here. Their response persuaded me that these things do have meaning for teachers and also that teachers are prepared to consider relatively difficult theoretical proposals in their search for ways of making the educational experiences of their students more worthwhile.

My thanks also to the many teachers who shared their work with me when many of the ideas expressed herein were germinating. Although I have held up your words for rigorous scrutiny, I appreciate and understand more fully now the nature of your endeavours to improve education.

To Stewart Bonser I say 'thank you' for your encouragement and critique which I value so highly.

Introduction

This book has its genesis in dissatisfaction with much of what is regarded as 'the gospel' of curriculum theory. This dissatisfaction was given focus when I took over the teaching of a course which examined the foundations of curriculum theory and found that the 'structure' of the curriculum and the 'foundations' were being confused. Aims and objectives, decision-making regarding content, implementation and evaluation strategies were all investigated as if these were the 'foundations' of the curriculum, rather than as one possible way of structuring a curriculum. It seemed that such a structure already presupposed a philosophical foundation which was never exposed. Moreover, the work of people such as Stenhouse has shown that it is possible to construct a curriculum differently from the traditional Tylerian (1949) model. When the curriculum is constructed in different ways does this mean that it has the same theoretical foundation? I suspected not, and in his work Stenhouse (1975) makes it quite explicit that he is building on different premises from those who work from, for instance, an objectives model.

There have been, of course, other more radical curriculum theorists who have proposed other theoretical foundations for the construction of curricula. I have found the work of Michael Apple (1979, 1982) and Henry Giroux (1981) of particular worth in this respect. That work shows that a Marxist critique can bring into question many of the assumptions of benign interest which we make of our education systems and our schools' curricula. But while the body of Marxist and Neo-Marxist educational critique provides us with a radical alternative as far as the foundations of curriculum theory are concerned, it often leaves the 'structure' of the alternative curriculum to the imagination. That is, it is not always easy to answer the question 'What will I do on Monday?' from the curriculum theorizing of the 'new left'.

Moreover, when I considered these various approaches to curriculum theory, it seemed that we were faced with three sets of foundations. All were different, and each would entail a different structuring of the curriculum. What was needed was a theoretical 'bedrock' which would provide a coherent 'foundation for the foundations' (the psychologists would probably say I was searching for a 'meta-foundation'). I found this coherent theory in Habermas' (1972) theory of knowledge-constitutive interests. It is, therefore, with an exploration of the implications of this theory for curriculum studies and practices that this book is concerned.

This is not the first attempt to make the link between Habermas' theories and educational theory. Carr and Kemmis (1986), for instance, provide an extensive exploration of the insights which Habermas' work can provide for educational research and that work could usefully be read in conjunction with this. Although Carr and Kemmis provide examples of the educational researching work of teachers, their analysis is not strongly grounded in the work of teachers. The claim that I would make for this present work is that it does attempt to ground the analysis strongly in the practice of teachers. I have done this, however, not simply to illustrate the theory through reference to practice, but rather to test the authenticity of the theory by placing it alongside the work of teachers. The conclusions which I draw from this exercise of examining the theory in the light of practice, however, can only function as proposals for you the reader, who must, in turn, subject these proposals to self-reflection in the light of your own curriculum experiences.

My agenda is to provide a coherent theoretical foundation for the work of curriculum deliberation and practice and, through that examination, to provide some proposals for the way in which the learning and teaching experiences of students and teachers might be improved.

Having set out that agenda, I would like to make some points about the audience for this work and for the way in which readers might approach it. Teachers who are engaged daily in the work of education are my target audience. There is a growing number of teachers who are wanting to find more meaning in their work. I meet them in university and in-service education courses, and it is primarily for these people that this labour has been undertaken. My colleagues in the academic community will no doubt also find this work of interest. However, it is the practitioner, not the theorist, with whom I am most concerned.

I realize that many of the ideas in this work will be new to these readers. Reflection upon my own history as a classroom teacher reminds me of how little opportunity teachers have to come into contact with ideas which have the potential to transform their work, as opposed to those which simply enhance or extend it. Reflection upon those classroom experiences causes me a twinge of regret that I did not have access to ideas which would have had the potential to help me understand some of the frustrations and contradictions I was experiencing. This work is presented to provide for teachers in similar situations a basis for understanding and for taking action to improve learning opportunities for their students.

With these intentions and considerations in mind, I have tried to present this work so that it does not have to be read from beginning to end. After the first chapter, each 'theoretical' chapter is followed by a 'practical' chapter. Readers who are new to many of these ideas might find that reading chapters 3, 5, 7 and 9 is a more productive way to commence. The more theoretical chapters may then be pursued later as familiarity and facility with the ideas grow.

It is important that theoretical explorations such as I undertake here are grounded in the realities of teachers' experiences. I am particularly grateful to Patrick Bertola who agreed to the inclusion here of the accounts of his classroom investigations. I have informally shared many of his insights with other teachers and am glad to have the opportunity of providing a wider audience for his writing. Apart from the work of Bertola and Cosgrove (whose writing is available elsewhere in the public domain), I have used pseudonyms for both teachers and projects.

The accounts of teachers' work cited in this book came from their writings concerning specific investigations of their own classroom practice. Most of these teachers also talked with me about these experiences during a series of interviews. These teachers did not write about their experiences with an academic audience in mind. Nevertheless, their writings are rich in insights about the foundations upon which teachers construct their curriculum practices. While I have subjected these writings and conversations to critical scrutiny, it is the message of the work, not the person, which is the subject of the critique. I admire the teachers whose work is represented here, as I do the many like them who care so much about teaching that they are willing to invest large amounts of personal time and energy in improving the educational experiences of their students.

These accounts are not, however, exemplary, nor do they 'prove' the theories that are explored in the following pages. The work of these teachers is presented as part of a set of critical theorems about curriculum theory and practice, and the reader is invited to test these propositions against personal knowledge and experience of curriculum, of the educational enterprise in general and visions of what might be.

Chapter 1

Three Fundamental Human Interests

Every educational practice implies a concept of man and the world.
(Freire, 1972b)

'Curriculum' is often written and spoken about in an idealistic sense as if there is a perfect 'idea' (*eidos*[1]) of a curriculum of which all individual curricula are more or less imperfect imitations. Thus, providing definitions of curriculum occupies the initial chapter of many a work on the subject. Curriculum, however, is not a concept; it is a cultural construction. That is, it is not an abstract concept which has some existence outside and prior to human experience. Rather, it is a way of organizing a set of human educational practices. I shall call these two ways of engaging in consideration of curriculum matters a conceptual and a cultural approach. To illustrate the difference between the two let us make an analogy with housing.

The conceptual approach to curriculum corresponds to a draughtsperson's approach to housing design. When draughting plans for a house it is important to recognize the parameters within which it is possible to design the house. There are certain minimum requirements if a construction is to be called a house, and it is the draughtsperson's responsibility to see that these basic requirements are met, and then, depending upon the situation of the client, that individual preferences are catered for. Out of the concept of a house, which is embedded in the consciousness of the draughtsperson and the expectations of the clients, as well as being embodied in the various regulations to which houses must conform, comes a set of plans which will guide the actions of the builders of the house (cf. Marsh and Stafford's, 1984, definition of curriculum as an 'interrelated set of plans and experiences . . .').

A cultural view of housing, however, would be more concerned with the houses in which people already live, the reasons for their living in such houses and what the house might be like should they wish to move into another. Some of the constructions into which people will want to move will be newly designed houses, so the concept of a house must be part of what will be examined when considering the culture of housing. But in general a cultural view of housing regards the house as part of the cultural life of the occupants or owners. Similarly, a cultural view of 'curriculum' is concerned with the experiences people have as a consequence of the existence of the curriculum, rather than with the various aspects which make it up.

This analogy also reminds us that very seldom do we start from 'scratch' in curriculum matters. Teachers and students are already engaged in curriculum practices. It is these which are of primary interest and it is these which will influence curriculum change. We might want to criticize some, perhaps many, of the curriculum practices we see in places of supposed learning. However, it is not productive to base such critique upon a failure of these practices to conform to some ideal, that is, the plans set out by the curriculum designers. Other foundations for understanding and providing a critique of curriculum practice must be found. It is with the provision of such foundations that this work is concerned.

The housing analogy highlights another important aspect of the way in which we must understand the curriculum; that is, it is a social construction. Writers reflecting a conceptual view of curriculum almost always acknowledge social influences upon curriculum design,[2] but usually in ways that suggest that, although such influences must be taken into account, the curriculum is, nevertheless, a logical deduction not a sociological construction. The curriculum of a society's schools is an integral part of the culture of that society. To understand the meaning of any set of curriculum practices, they must be seen as both arising out of a set of historical circumstances and as being a reflection of a particular social milieu.

As with any analogy, the housing metaphor cannot be pushed too far and this one becomes misleading to the extent that it encourages the tendency to think of the curriculum as a 'thing'. Talking about curriculum is another way of talking about the educational practices of certain institutions. This means that it is not on the teacher's shelf that one looks for the curriculum, but in the actions of the people engaged in education. The question 'What is curriculum?' is, thus, more like the question 'What is football?' than 'What is hydrogen?' That is, to think about curriculum is to think about how a group of people act and interact in certain situations. It is not to describe and analyze an element which exists apart from human interaction.

We shall not pursue the game analogy too far, but seeing curriculum as more like football than hydrogen enables us to understand what is meant by 'social construction'. With hydrogen, we need to know only about the nature of the element itself in order to understand it. We do not, for instance, need to know about the balloon which it is filling to understand the element itself. But with football, we need to know about the society in which it is being played to know about the nature of the game. Hydrogen is the same whether it is found in London or Sydney, but football isn't. So also with the curriculum. No curriculum has an a priori existence. If we are to understand the meaning of the curriculum practices engaged in by people in a society, we need to know about the social context of the school. But we not only need to know about the composition and organization of the society; we also need to understand the fundamental premises upon which it is constructed. The fact that we can talk sensibly about the curriculum of the Athenian Academy and of Soviet schools means only that we can use a word in an appropriate context. There is nothing in the nature of 'curriculum' as such that would give us any inkling about what might constitute such curricula. To make anything other than random guesses about the curriculum of any institution, we need to know, not about the nature of curriculum per se, but rather about the context of the institution.

Such an assertion brings us to the quotation at the beginning of this chapter that 'every educational practice implies a concept of man and the world.' Educational practices, and the curriculum is one set of these, do not exist apart from beliefs about people and the way in which they do and ought to interact in the world. If we scratch the surface of educational practice, and that implies organizational as well as teaching and learning practices, we find, not universal natural laws, but beliefs and values. The question to be asked then is, 'What sorts of beliefs about persons and the world will lead to the construction of what educational practices, particularly the educational practices which are encompassed by the term "curriculum"?'

The Theory of Cognitive Interests

A framework for making meaning of curriculum practices is provided by the theory of 'knowledge–constitutive interests' proposed by the German philosopher Jürgen Habermas. This is a theory about the fundamental human interests which influence how knowledge is 'constituted' or constructed. Even providing this brief explanation of the premises of this present work reveals an implied 'concept of man and the world'. A view that knowledge exists somehow apart from people and is 'discovered' by them is not what is being accepted here. Rather, knowledge is recognized as being something which people together construct.

Habermas has been described in the following way by Thomas McCarthy, one of the translators of much of his work:

> Jürgen Habermas is the dominant figure on the intellectual scene in Germany today.... There is scarcely an area of the humanities or social sciences that has not felt the influence of his thought. (1978, p. ix).

This influence is beginning to be felt in the English-speaking world, although until recently his impact upon educational theory was negligible. His theoretical explorations into the nature of human knowledge and theory/practice relationships were not written within a context of educational theory, nor do they arise directly out of educational considerations. They do, however, have implications for educational theory and for understanding educational practices.

The main works in which Habermas explores the theory of cognitive interests are *Knowledge and Human Interests* (1972) and *Theory and Practice* (1974). *Towards a Rational Society* (1971) provides an analysis of human action which is important for understanding the cognitive interests. These publication dates are of English translations; publication in German occurred a number of years prior to that in English.

To understand these theoretical proposals for the foundations of human knowledge and action, it is necessary to comprehend initially what Habermas means by 'interest', and then what a cognitive interest is.

Interests

Interest in general is the pleasure that we connect with the existence of an object or an action. (Habermas, 1972, p. 198)

What Habermas means by 'interest' arises out of a reconstruction of the analysis of interest undertaken by his philosophical forebears.[3] He proceeds from the premise that the basic orientation of the human species is towards pleasure and that fundamentally what gives us pleasure is the creation of the conditions which will enable the species to reproduce itself. It might be supposed that the creation of conditions for the species to continue its survival implies a view of the human person as a sensual being, perhaps akin to the Freudian Id. For Habermas, however, the creation of these conditions is rooted and grounded in rationality. This implies that the highest and purest forms of pleasure are to be experienced in rationality. The most fundamental interest of the human species, therefore, is an interest in rationality.

Earlier philosophers, such as Fichte and Kant, who had considered this question of fundamental human interests and had also concluded that fundamentally human interests were rational, had deduced the notion of pure rational interest logically. Habermas has looked to the evolution of the human species itsef in order to authenticate the theory of rationality. He argues that what separates the human being from its evolutionary forebears is the act of speech. It is within the speech act, the very act which determines 'humanness', that the interest in rationality is discernible.[4] Geuss (1981) has summarized Habermas' position in the following way:

> To be a human agent ... is to participate at least potentially in a speech community ... but no agent can be potentially a member of a speech community who cannot recognize the difference between true and false statements in some general way. (p. 65)

Interests, in general, are *fundamental orientations of the human species* and pure interests are fundamental, rational orientations. This does not mean just that human beings have a fundamental orientation towards rationality, but rather that the fundamental interest in 'the preservation of life is rooted in life organized through knowledge [as well as] action' (1972, p. 211). Put simply, even something as basic as the survival of the human species is not a matter of instinct and random behaviours. It is grounded in knowledge and human action.

But Habermas goes further than simply proposing that there is a relationship between the fundamental orientation of the species towards preservation of life and knowledge (or rationality). He asserts that the way in which that orientation works itself out in the life structures of the species will determine what counts as knowledge. That is, rationality can be applied in a number of different ways to ensure self-preservation. The manner in which rationality manifests itself will determine what a social group is prepared to distinguish as knowledge. So, not only do fundamental interests in preservation have cognitive as well as practical implications, but those interests will also constitute knowledge in different ways. Thus, the pure interest in reason expresses itself in the form of three knowledge-constitutive interests.

These knowledge-constitutive interests do not merely represent an orientation *towards* knowledge or rationality on the part of the human species, but rather constitute human knowledge itself. Richard Bernstein (1979, p. 192) explains: 'such interests or orientations are *knowledge-constitutive* because they *shape and determine* what counts as the objects and types of knowledge' (emphasis mine). Knowledge-constitutive interests both shape what we consider to constitute knowledge and determine the categories by which we organize that knowledge.

Technical, Practical and Emancipatory Interests

Habermas identifies three basic cognitive interests: technical, practical and emancipatory. These interests constitute the three types of science by which knowledge is generated and organized in our society. These three ways of knowing are empirical-analytic, historical-hermeneutic and critical:

> The task of the empirical-analytic sciences incorporates a technical cognitive interest; that of the historical-hermeneutic sciences incorporates a practical interest and the approach of critically oriented sciences incorporates the emancipatory cognitive interest. (1972, p. 308)

It is important to remember that in the preservation and reproduction of the species knowledge alone is insufficient. Knowledge and action together constitute the life structures of the species. This is an important point, for it indicates that neither knowledge nor action is sufficient of itself to ensure preservation. Both must interact for the welfare of the species. Therefore, although Habermas has emphasized the role that these interests play in constructing knowledge, they could also be called 'action-constitutive' interests (1972, p. 211). This becomes important when we consider curriculum as a social construction which is part of the life structure of a society. Both knowledge and action as they interact in educational practice are determined by a particular cognitive interest.

The Technical Interest

The technical interest, like each of the fundamental human interests, is grounded in the need of the species to survive and reproduce both itself and those aspects of human society which are deemed to be of most worth. To achieve this purpose, persons have a basic orientation towards controlling and managing the environment. This orientation is what Habermas calls the technical interest (1972, p. 309).

Habermas identifies this interest as being congruent with the agenda of the empirical-analytic sciences.[5] The type of knowledge generated by empirical-analytic science is grounded in experience and observation, often produced through experimentation. Theories associated with such science 'comprise hypothetico-deductive connections of propositions, which permit the deduction of lawlike hypotheses with empirical content' (1972, p. 308).

This is the form of knowledge known as 'positivism', the term coined by Compte, one of the early advocates of this way of producing and organizing knowledge. Habermas describes Compte's semantic analysis of the word 'positivism' which provides a succinct contrast between objectivity and subjectivity: 'Compte ... uses "positive" to refer to the actual in contrast to the merely imaginary ... what can claim certainty in contrast to the undecided ... the exact in contrast to the indefinite ... what claims relative validity in contrast to the absolute' (1972, p. 74). For the empirical-analytic sciences, then, knowledge consists of certain theories about the world which are grounded in our 'positive' observation and experience of that world.

But empirical-analytic knowledge comprises more than an infinite number of isolated observations or experiences. This knowledge is structured according to series of hypotheses by which meaning is made of observations and which also have predictive power. Prediction allows us to anticipate what the environment (probably) will be like tomorrow based upon our experience of what it is like today. It also allows us, potentially, to control our environment based upon that knowledge. 'The meaning of such predictions', claims Habermas, 'is their technical exploitability.'

There is general agreement amongst philosophers of science (both the advocates of and detractors from positivism) about the centrality of prediction in empirical-analytic science. The assertion that prediction means control, however, is one to which there might be objections. What is assumed in such an assertion is that there is a relationship between knowledge and power and between science and technology. That is, that knowledge is power. Habermas is making a stronger claim, however, than that there is a possible relationship between prediction and control. For Habermas the fundamental interest which guides empirical-analytic science is an interest in control and the technical exploitability of knowledge (the technical cognitive interest).

This view of science means that what counts as knowledge in the empirical-analytic sciences is governed by a fundamental human interest in explaining, explanations providing the basis for prediction and predictions providing the basis for the control of the environment. Explanations are deductively (or logically) possible from hypothetical statements. They are then able to be empirically verified through observation.

The technical interest gives rise to a certain form of action. This is instrumental action which is 'governed by technical rules based upon empirical knowledge' (1971, p. 91). Since empirical-analytic science is concerned with identifying the regularities that exist in the environment, it is then possible to formulate rules for action based upon these regularities. This is presumably the premise behind much educational research. If we can discover, through observation and experimentation, the 'laws' which govern how pupils learn, we can presumably structure a set of rules which, if followed, will promote learning. So, if we discover that positive reinforcement is a regular factor in learning to read, a set of rules about the application of positive reinforcement will presumably lead to pupils learning to read.

Put succinctly, the technical interest is: *a fundamental interest in controlling the environment through rule-following action based upon empirically grounded laws.* Just what such an interest means for curriculum will be explored in greater detail in the following chapter. There it will be argued that the objectives model of curriculum design is informed by a technical cognitive interest. This means that implicit within objectives models of curriculum, such as Tyler's (1949), is an interest in controlling pupil learning so that, at the end of the teaching process, the product will conform to the *eidos* (that is, the intentions or ideas) expressed in the original objectives.

The Practical Interest

The basic orientation of the technical interest is towards control, but that of the practical interest is towards understanding (1972, p. 310). This is not, however, technical understanding. It is not the sort of understanding which enables rules to be formulated so that the environment may be manipulated and managed. Rather, it is an interest in understanding the environment so that one is able to interact with it. The practical interest is grounded in the fundamental need of the human species to live in and as part of the world, not to be, as it were, in competition with the environment for survival.

As soon as the move is made into the realm of understanding in order to survive 'along with', one moves more obviously into the moral sphere. I say 'more obviously' because there is a moral position implicit in the technical interest, but it is often disguised in talk about 'objectivity' and 'natural law'. The question motivated by a practical interest becomes not 'What can I do?', but 'What ought I to do?' To answer this question, understanding of the meaning of the situation is required. That is why this interest is called the 'practical' interest — it is an interest in taking right action ('practical' action) within a particular environment.

The production of knowledge through the making of meaning is the task associated with the historical-hermeneutic sciences. Within the gamut of these sciences fall historical and literary interpretation and the interpretative agendas of such disciplines as sociology and some branches of psychology. Habermas says of these forms of knowledge:

> The historical-hermeneutic sciences gain knowledge in a different methodological framework. Here the meaning of the validity of propositions is not constituted in the frame of reference of technical control. . . . Theories are not constructed deductively and experience is not organized with regard to the success of operations. Access to the facts is provided by the understanding of meaning, not observation. The verification of lawlike hypotheses in the empirical-analytic sciences has its counterpart here in the interpretation of texts. (1972, p. 309)

The notion of 'texts' here is interesting. It is clear how one might bring interpretation to bear on an historical document to make meaning of it, but the interpretation of actions is another matter. Both empirical and interpretative sciences have to transform human action into something else to study it. The empirical-analytic sciences turn it into 'behaviour', breaking down action into small 'manageable' parts to experiment with and the analyze. Interpretative sciences want to deal with action in a more holistic sense, so they find ways of recording action and later reproducing it in some form; it might be in the form of field notes, photographs or audio or video recordings. In this way the action is reproduced as a text and so can be interpreted in similar ways as can other forms of textual material.[6]

Knowledge which is concerned with understanding is not to be judged according to the success of the operations arising as a consequence of that knowledge. Rather, it is to be judged according to whether the interpreted meaning assisted the process of making judgments about how to act rationally and morally.[7] Such action, however, is not objective action; that is, it is not action upon an 'object' or even upon a person who has been 'objectified'. It is subjective action; that is, it is the action of a subject in the universe acting with another subject.

The action which arises as a consequence of this interest is, therefore, 'interaction' which Habermas defines in the following way:

> By interaction ... I understand Communicative action, symbolic interaction. It is governed by binding consensual norms, which define reciprocal expectations of behaviour, and which must be understood and recognized by at least two acting subjects. (1971, p. 92)

Interaction is not action *upon* an environment which has been objectified (that is, is regarded as an object); it is action *with* the environment (organic or human), which is regarded as a subject in the interaction. Similarly, the knowledge which guides such action is subjective, not objective. This is what is meant when Habermas says, 'access to the facts is provided by the understanding of meaning, not observation.' Although such knowledge is subjective, this does not mean that it is arbitrary. Confidence in an interpretation depends upon agreement with others that such an interpretation is reasonable, hence Habermas' claim above regarding the necessity for agreement between 'at least two acting subjects'. Thus, the notion of consensus is an important one with respect to the interpretation of meaning.

The practical interest is, therefore, the interest which generates subjective rather than objective knowledge (that is, knowledge of the world as subject rather than knowledge of the world as object). This interest could be defined in the following way: *the practical interest is a fundamental interest in understanding the environment through interaction based upon a consensual interpretation of meaning.*

The key concepts associated with the practical cognitive interest are understanding and interaction. When we consider the implications of a practical interest for curriculum, these same concepts are central. A curriculum informed by a practical interest is not a means-end curriculum by which an educational outcome is produced through the action of a teacher upon a group of objectified pupils. Rather, curriculum design is regarded as a process through which pupil and teacher interact in order to make meaning of the world. Stenhouse claims:

> The infant class considering the origins of a playground fight and the historian considering the origins of the First World War are essentially engaged in the same sort of task. They are attempting to understand both the event and the concept by which they seek to explicate it. (1975, p. 85)

Stenhouse's process model of curriculum will be examined in a later chapter as an example of a proposal for curriculum design informed by a practical interest.

It follows from the moral imperative associated with the practical interest that curriculum informed by such an interest will be concerned, not simply with promoting knowledge in pupils, but also with promoting right action. This could be implied from Stenhouse's example of the infant class, but is it also true of the history classroom?

Habermas claims that the link between understanding and action is the hermeneutic concept of application.[8] Application is not, however, an optional link between understanding and acting (that is, we do not just act as a consequence of applying understanding gained from one situation to another). Rather, we cannot fully understand any given situation unless we apply it to ourselves:

> Hermeneutic knowledge is always mediated through … pre-understanding, which is derived from the interpreter's initial situation. The world of traditional meaning discloses itself to the interpreter only to the extent that his own world becomes clarified at the same time…. He comprehends the substantive content of tradition by applying tradition to himself and his situation. (1972, pp. 309–10)

Application in this sense is a subjective process. So also curriculum proposals which are informed by a practical interest do not shun subjectivity, but rather acknowledge the centrality of judgment. 'A process model [of curriculum development]', says Stenhouse, 'rests on teacher judgment, rather than teacher direction' (1975, p. 96).

The Emancipatory Interest

The emancipatory interest is perhaps the hardest of these conceptual categories to grasp, but it is in the identification of this interest that

Habermas has made his most original contribution to modern philosophy.

Although interests are 'fundamental orientations' of the human species, they can themselves be categorized either as being stimulated by inclination or by principles of reason. In common language we would usually associate interest with inclination. If the claim is then made that human persons are motivated by fundamental interest, this might be interpreted as indicating a belief in the ultimate non-rationality of persons. It is important to realize that interests can also be stimulated by principles of reason. Following on from Kant, Habermas views persons as intrinsically, or at least potentially, rational beings, so interests which are stimulated by reason are more fundamental than interests which are stimulated by inclination or desire (1972, pp. 198ff).

Given what amounts to a hierarchy of interests, we may ask, 'What is it that Habermas sees as the fundamental, "pure" interest?' (that is, pure in the sense of being grounded in reason). It is an interest in emancipation (1972, pp. 205ff). Emancipation for Habermas means 'independence from all that is outside the individual' and is a state of autonomy rather than libertinism. Thus Habermas identifies emancipation with autonomy and responsibility (*Mündigeit*). It is only in the act of self-reflection (that is, as the ego turns in upon itself) that emancipation is possible. Although emancipation must ultimately be an individual experience if it is to have any reality, it is not simply an individual matter. Because of the interactive nature of human society, individual freedom can never be separated from the freedom of others. Hence emancipation is also inextricably linked with notions of justice and ultimately with equality. But these are complex relationships which we will take up later.

If the fundamental pure interest of persons is in emancipation, the question must arise: 'Emancipation from what?' Habermas (1972, p. 208) explains:

> Self-reflection is at once intuition and emancipation, comprehension and liberation from dogmatic dependence. The dogmatism that reason undoes … is false-consciousness: error and unfree existence in particular. Only the ego that apprehends itself … as the self-positing subject obtains autonomy. The dogmatist … lives in dispersal as a dependent subject that is not only determined by objects but is itself made into a thing.

This is a powerful image of the unfree, 'objectified' person, at the mercy of false-consciousness, juxtaposed with the autonomous subject, heeding the Platonic injunction to 'Know thyself!' We must ask the question, however, 'Are not the technical and practical interests capable of fulfilling the human orientation towards autonomy and responsibility?' The answer is 'no'. The technical interest will not facilitate autonomy and responsibility because it is an interest in control. An interest in control will certainly facilitate independence for some, but this is false autonomy, for it is an 'autonomy' which entails regarding fellow humans and/or the environment as objects. This is the sort of freedom which arises out of a Darwinian 'survival of the fittest' world view or fundamentalist views that the earth was given to *man*kind to subdue and rule. The technical interest is one which arises from inclination, not from reason.

The practical interest will not suffice either, although it comes closer to serving the interests of autonomy and responsibility. Through the practical interest the universe is regarded as subject, not object, and there is a potential for freedom through the emphasis upon consensual meaning and understanding. But the practical interest proves to be inadequate for the promotion of true emancipation precisely because of the propensity of persons to be deceived, even when understandings are arrived at in open discussion and debate. The operation of consensus politics under the Australian Hawke government is an example of the potential for consensual meaning to become a form of dogmatism rather than promoting autonomy. It became clear in the early 'summit' meeting (convened shortly after the Labour government came to power) that it was ultimately the opinions of the powerful in the society around which consensus was formed. The resulting 'agreements' had all the more power because they were made in a situation of supposed open debate. However laudatory may be the objective of consensus arrived at through open debate and deliberation, the suspicion arises that consensus can be used as a form of manipulation. Even when it does not consciously operate as manipulation, there is the possibility of the participants deceiving themselves about the real meaning of a situation. This critiques is not made to deny the value of consensus, but to illustrate that consensus can be false when powerful interests are participating in the meaning-making and agreement process.

So neither fundamental orientations towards technical nor practical reasoning will ensure that the even more fundamental interest in autonomy and responsibility will be served. There must be an interest in freeing persons from the coercion of the technical and the possible deceit of the practical. This is the interest in emancipation, the so-called emancipatory interest.

When Habermas writes of the emancipatory interest being a fundamental human interest, he is not making a value judgment based upon some view of human nature as something which is 'given' to persons or 'ordained'. Rather, he sees emancipation as an evolutionary principle being implicit in the very act of speech which separates persons from other forms of life.

The idea of freedom, the so-called emancipatory cognitive interest, is not ontological in the sense of being an inalienable aspect of human nature. Rather, it is transcendental in that it is implicit in human interaction. It is not transcendental, however, in the sense of existing independently of human society. Emancipation is not an *eidos* which, like Plato's Forms, exists in the heavens to be imitated in human society. It is implicit in the very act of speech; speech being the attribute which has separated man from his evolutionary forebears. Geuss (1981, p. 65) summarizes Habermas' position:

> To be a human agent ... is to participate at least potentially in a speech community ... but no agent can ever be potentially a member of a speech community who cannot recognize the difference between true and false statements in some general way ... but what it means for a statement to be true is that it would be one on which all agents would agree if they were to discuss all of human experience in absolutely free and un-coerced circumstances for an indefinite period of time.

We may say, therefore, that one of the basic orientations of persons is towards freedom, and we can know that such is the case because the notion of freedom is fundamental to the act of speech and to understanding, for which speech exists. Interestingly, the concept of freedom is inextricably linked with interests in truth and justice.

So, we may ask, how does the emancipatory interest translate into action in the real world? The emancipatory interest gives rise to autonomous, responsible action based upon prudent decisions informed by a certain kind of knowledge. The knowledge generated by an emancipatory interest exists at a number of levels. Firstly, the emancipatory interest generates *critical theories*. These are theories about persons and about society which explain how coercion and distortion operate to inhibit freedom. Freudian psychology is one example of a critical theory about the inhibition of freedom in individuals; Marxism is an example of a critical theory about the inhibition of freedom in whole societies; and various theories of ideology also address the problem of how interaction can be distorted or coerced by certain interests. Certain strands of Christianity are also developing critical theories, for example, liberation theology. But theories are not enough. Critical theory must be authenticated for each individual or group. That is, groups must be able to say not only 'yes, we are convinced that this is true', but also 'yes, that is also true for us!' Authentication takes place through processes of self-reflection. So, the other type of knowledge generated by the emancipatory interest is *authentic insight*.

While the other two interests are concerned with control and understanding respectively, the emancipatory interest is concerned with *empowerment*, that is, the ability of individuals and groups to take control of their own lives in autonomous and responsible ways. The emancipatory cognitive interest could be defined as follows: *a fundamental interest in emancipation and empowerment to engage in autonomous action arising out of authentic, critical insights into the social construction of human society*.

Again, we must make the link with curriculum. What does it mean for curriculum to be informed by an emancipatory interest? To understand emancipatory curriculum, we must grasp the shortcomings of the practical orientation. As was seen previously, the problem with viewing curriculum as a meaning-making process is that we may be deceived as to the true meaning of events. If true emancipation is to occur, it is important that the subject be freed from 'false consciousness'. Thus, an emancipatory curriculum will work towards freedom on a number of levels. First of all, at the level of consciousness, the subjects participating in the educational experience will come to know theoretically and in terms of their own existence when propositions represent distorted views of the world (views which serve interests in domination) and when they represent invariant regularities of existence. At the level of practice, the emancipatory curriculum will involve the participants in the educational encounter, both teacher and pupil, in action which attempts to change the structures within which learning occurs and which constrain freedom in often unrecognized ways. An emancipatory curriculum entails a reciprocal relationship between self-reflection and action.

Although fundamental, these relationships are complex ones to grasp. They need to be understood against the backcloth of the other cognitive interests and the implications which these have for the curriculum. The most important principle to acknowledge from this overview of the cognitive interests is that curriculum is a social construction. Furthermore, the form and purposes of that construction will be determined by some fundamental human interests which imply concepts of persons and their world.

Notes

1   The Greek word *eidos* can roughly be translated 'idea', but the Greek concept encompasses an assemblage of English terms including such concepts as plan, pattern, design, recipe and concept.
2   Such social influence is sometimes regretted. Hirst and Peters (1970, p. 110), for instance, speak disparagingly of students and teachers who are 'bound to be affected by the motivations of the wider society.'
3   Reconstruction is a particularly German form of theorizing. It does not involve reinterpreting a theory, but rather taking the premises of the theorists and developing the argument as it ought to have been developed if the theorist had not made errors at certain key points.
4   We will see later that rationality is inextricably linked with freedom in Habermas' thought, and both truth and freedom are implicit in the speech act.
5   For an easily understood account of the nature of empirical-analytic science see chalmers, A.F. (1976) *What Is This Thing Called Science?*
6   For further exploration of the idea of action as text see Ricoeur (1979).
7   In chapter 9 of *Knowledge and Human Interests* Habermas reconstructs the theories of Kant and Fichte in order to explore the connection between reason and morality.
8   For an exploration of the hermeneutic concept of application see Gadamer (1979), pp. 274ff.

Chapter 2

Curriculum as Product

A teacher who had joined one of my courses came to me feeling rather agitated after a session in which we had been exploring some of the ideas canvassed in the previous chapter. 'I'm feeling really angry', she exclaimed, 'I have been working in what I considered to be unique ways in my classroom for many years, and now I find that there is this body of theory and all I have been doing all along is applying someone else's theories!'

Of course, she had not been 'applying' the theory at all. She was now simply authenticating it as she engaged in a process of self-reflection through which she tested the theoretical explanation in the light of her own experience. If the technical, practical and emancipatory interests are indeed 'fundamental' to the human species, we would expect to find people already acting in ways which were congruent with the theory, but they are not acting *because* of the theory. Furthermore, taking action which is informed by a technical, a practical or an emancipatory interest is not simply a matter of 'applying the theory'. The critical theorems of Habermas offer a set of possible interpretations of action by providing a basis for understanding the way in which the knowledge underlying action is constructed. They do not provide a blueprint for action if, for example, we want to change from acting in a technical way to taking practical action. Furthermore, if these are fundamental human interests, and not simply identifiable ways of acting in the twentieth century, then we would expect that these interests have been informing human action for a long time. In fact people have also been theorizing about these ways of acting for a long time. In a moment we shall leave the twentieth century theoretical propositions of Habermas and revisit the fifth century B.C. ideas of Aristotle to explore these concepts further.

As we saw in the previous chapter, Habermas claims that these interests are fundamental to the human species. He claims further that their fundamental nature is not simply discernible through an examination of the way in which people act now. Rather, these knowledge-constitutive interests are identifiable through a reconstruction of the evolution of the human species (Habermas, 1979). By this he means that to be convinced about the authenticity of the theory of cognitive interests, we do not have to resort to abstract philosophical debate. If we reconstruct the evolution of the species, particularly the development of the act of speech, the fundamental cognitive interests are discernible. Habermas' insistence on the reconstruction of the evolution of the species, rather than an appeal to ancient philosophies as the way to understanding the nature of the concept of interest, may be philosophically more commendable and more rationally convincing, however, the argument is long and complex. I would encourage readers who are interested in pursuing the argument from first principles to consider the theory of communicative competence as it is outlined in Habermas' (1979) *Communication and the Evolution of Society*. For our purposes of understanding the relevance of the theory of cognitive interest to the business of curriculum, we will depend upon the ancients, in particular Aristotle. Although Aristotle did not use the Habermasian concept of interests, he identified technical and practical human dispositions, and it is possible to match Aristotle's dispositions with the Habermasian technical and practical interests.

Aristotle and the Technical Interest

In the *Nicomachean Ethics* Aristotle examines the whole question of ethics via a consideration of different kinds of human action and the dispositions which inform action. The disposition which informs one kind of human action is the disposition *techne* or skill. This is the disposition which Aristotle identifies as being associated with the action of the craftsman. (Rather than using the somewhat laborious form craftsperson, I shall adopt the more gender-neutral term 'artisan' for what is usually translated from Aristotle as 'craftsman'.) The action in which the artisan engages is called *poietike*, in English 'making' action. It is from the Greek *poietike* that the English word 'poetry' comes. *Poietike* means 'creating' in the artistic sense of creating a play or a sculpture as well as 'making' in the more mechanical sense of making a cake or building a bridge.

This form of action, which is dependent upon the exercising of skill *(techne),* always results from the idea, image or pattern of what the artisan wants to make. (In the Greek all of these words are represented by the term *eidos. Eidos* is like the English term 'idea' but encompasses this wider range of meanings.) Although skilled actions may allow for some decision-making and choice, the range of choice, and hence the freedom that the artisan has to take action, is always restricted by the *eidos* of what is to be created. Thus the poet may have a choice of words or the carpenter make decisions about what materials to use, but those decisions will always be determined by the *eidos* of what is to be created. Decisions about particular actions will also depend upon the level of skill possessed by the artisan, and it is in this area of his/her work that the artisan generally has most control. As skills are improved, a greater range of options within which choices can be made becomes available, but those options are quite finite. The *eidos* will restrict the range of choices available to the artisan. For example, a dressmaker might be exceedingly skilled in the art of making button holes, but if the pattern calls for a zip fastener, her choice of exercising her skill of button-holing is limited. (That is, unless she is both designer and maker and can change the pattern). Or, to take an example closer to our concerns, a teacher may be very skilled in teaching 'times tables' using a variety of rote learning methods. When she teaches, she exercises her choice among methods. However, if a new syllabus document is developed which requires the learning of number facts through other than rote methods, our teacher's range of teaching options is limited.

The sort of decision-making which is involved in deciding which of our skills we will apply in a particular situation Habermas calls 'strategic' action. In *Towards a Rational Society* he says, 'Strategic action depends upon the correct evaluation of possible alternative choices' (1971, p. 92). Such ability is itself a *techne*. Strategic action, as its military connotations remind us, is always taken to achieve certain predetermined and quite specific objectives. So the choice of a particular skill to apply in a situation will be determined by the end which is to be achieved.

When action is informed by a technical interest (that is, the disposition of *techne*), therefore, it is constituted by a number of elements. These are the *eidos* (the guiding idea) and the *techne* (the guiding disposition) which together provide the basis for *poietike* ('making' action). The relationships between these various components are expressed diagrammatically in Figure 1. Although I have resorted to a diagram here, I am mindful of Barrow's scepticism that models and diagrams 'are "clothes" that disguise the Emperor's nakedness' (1984, p. 61). Representing educational ideas in graphic form reduces 'educational issues [to] mechanical and technological terms.' In this case, however, since my claim is that the technical interest does represent a form of mechanical action (the propensity of artisans to be replaced by machines reminds us just how mechanical such action is), it is probably appropriate that the dynamics of action arising out of a technical interest be presented in just such a way.

In Figure 1 the components of 'making' action are represented in a linear relationship. The *eidos* can only come into being through the *techne* (skill) of the practitioner, but, in turn, it is the *eidos* which prescribes the nature of the product, not the artisan's skill. The outcome of *poietike* (making action) is, thus, some product. This does not mean that the product will always replicate the *eidos*. The artisan's skill may be deficient or chance factors may be at work. The product will be judged, however, according to the extent to which it 'measures up' to the image implicit in the guiding *eidos*.

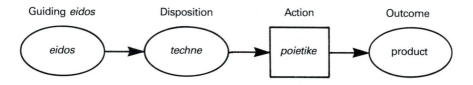

Figure 1. *The Technical Relationship of Ideas and Actions*

Let us apply this analysis to the actions of artisans in the building of a house. The *eidos* (plan or design) comes from the architect and it is through the skills of the various artisans that their actions transform the *eidos* into the reality of a standing house. The plans may be modified during construction and lack of skill may mean that the outcome of the worker's actions is not the 'poetry in masonry' that the owners envisaged, but the basic relationship of idea, skill and action remains.

But is it possible to regard a curriculum as a production exercise in a similar way? We would need to be able to apply this analysis in a similar way if the Aristotelian concepts of *techne* and *poietike* are to have any application to the curriculum enterprise. When we look at how the concept of curriculum is portrayed in much of the literature and how it is understood through curriculum design practices, it is possible to discern an implicit technical interest. Take, for example, the following definitions of curriculum:

An interrelated set of plans and experiences which a student completes under the guidance of the school. (Marsh and Stafford, 1984, p. 3)

All the planned experiences provided by the school to assist the pupils in attaining the designated learning outcomes to the best of their abilities. (Neagley and Evan, 1967)

A programme of activities (by teachers and pupils) designed so that pupils will attain so far as possible certain educational and other schooling ends or objectives. (Barrow, 1984, p. 11)

Note in these definitions of curriculum the importance of the *eideis* (plans, programmes). They will exist prior to and outside the learning experiences which constitute the child's schooling. It will be through the teacher's skill that the curriculum plan or learning objectives will be implemented to bring about the desired learning in the pupil. The teaching action in which the teacher engages in this form of curriculum implementation is 'making' action (*poietike*). This implies that the teaching act is product oriented. We may ask, however, 'What is the product of such a curriculum?' All of the above definitions suggest that the product of the application of the curriculum is the student. Moreover, it is quite commonplace to hear talk of 'the products of our educational system', meaning the students who come through the system. Some of these products are numerate or literate children, good citizens, or perhaps effective communicators. Sometimes the outcome of the implementation of a set of curriculum plans is not envisaged in terms of human product, but is oriented to a material product, perhaps a well written essay, correctly computed sets of calculations, or interesting pieces of art work.

In all cases where education is regarded in this product oriented sense, the teacher is required to exercise his/her skill to reproduce in the realm of the classroom some *eidos*. That *eidos* may be inherent in the expected work practices of the teachers; for example, the fact that teachers are expected to keep order implies a guiding *eidos* of orderly, well behaved student products coming out of the schooling system. The 'images' of what the students will become as a result of receiving the skilled attentions of the teacher are also represented in various curriculum documents and syllabus statements. This could be called a reproductive view of curriculum. It is a view which suggests that the purpose of a teacher's work is to reproduce in the students the various *eideis* which guide that work.

It is important for us to realize that when teachers work in a way which is analogous to the way in which artisans work, their work is essentially reproductive, not productive. That is, they are not being creative or productive in an autonomous sense; they are reproducing in the material world *eideis* which already exist in the abstract world of ideas or which have already been reproduced elsewhere. This notion of the reproductive function of education has become important in educational theory in recent years and has implications beyond simply providing explanations of the nature of teachers' work.

The part played by schools in cultural reproduction has achieved some attention from sociologists of education in recent times. This concept has developed importance in educational debate following Althusser's (1972) Marxist analysis of the ideologically reproductive functions of various 'state apparatuses', one of which is schooling. In the English-speaking world the concept of reproduction has been applied to education in such analyses as the mid-seventies work of Bowles and Gintis (1976) who argued that the function of schools is to reproduce the class divisions of capitalist society. The reproduction thesis addresses the power relationships which exist in societies and argues, to put it in a very simplified and therefore rather crass form, that although certain artefacts of a culture may change as its history develops, there is a continuity in the power relationships of a society (particularly in capitalist society). This continuity is not a result of chance. Rather, the existing power relationships of one historical moment are reproduced in another through various social practices and forms of organization. Education is one such important structure and ensemble of practices which performs this reproductive function.

The early conceptualization of reproduction in educational theory has been labelled by Apple (1979) as a 'mechanistic' portrayal of the social function of schooling. A simplistic understanding of the notion of reproduction has also been attacked by other educational theorists, not least because a strict application of the conception of reproduction allows no space for social change or improvement (cf. Green, 1986). That is, if we contend that groups within each generation of a society have a vested interest in ensuring that the power structures of that society remain unaltered so that the power and influence which they have remains into the following generation, it is difficult to account for any social change which is not a result of an oppressed group seizing power. Of course, sometimes social change occurs in this way, but often it occurs more gradually. Nevertheless, schooling does have a reproductive function. It is part of what schools are about to pass on the mores and traditions of a society so that the social structure is maintained. This reproductive function is one of the consequences of the technical cognitive interest, the interest in survival through control and manipulation of the environment.

The technical interest presupposes a hierarchical relationship between theory and practice. Practices exist in order to bring certain plans to fulfilment. Moreover, good practice is taken to be evidence of sound theory. Robin Barrow claims that:

> Good practice logically presupposes theory, as a good bridge presupposes scientific theory and a good painting theory of art, in the sense that the goodness in question is a matter of the bridge or painting matching up to theoretical requirements. (1984, p. 13)

Note the technical metaphors here of bridges and paintings (technical in the Aristotelian sense). Implicit is the principle of theory presupposing practice and of any judgments about the product being in terms of the theory (the *eidos*). This representation of the theory-practice relationship is very Platonic. Plato believed that there were Forms or Ideas of every material thing or human attribute existing in 'the heavens', and that every earthly instance was a mere reproduction of the heavenly Form (*Republic*, Book X). It is to get away from such metaphysical explanations of the human condition that Habermas seeks confirmation of his theoretical position in the reconstruction of human evolution. It is significant that elements of this technical representation of human knowledge and action are present in many facets and phases of human understanding.

To understand further the implications of the technical interest for curriculum theory and practice, we will consider two important aspects of the curriculum construction process: the notion of curriculum design and the implications which that has for the control of the curriculum.

Curriculum Design

One interesting way of detecting a technical interest is to identify the metaphors or analogies by which human activities are described. To speak of 'constructing' or 'designing' curriculum is itself to speak in metaphor and to use a technical metaphor at that. Talk about 'curriculum design' is usually indicative of a technical interest.

Tyler (1949), one of the founding fathers of the modern curriculum movement, is credited with providing a blueprint for the curriculum design process. He disclaims that such was his purpose in *Basic Principles of Curriculum and Construction*. The way in which he speaks about curriculum practices in the Introduction to that work provides evidence that a technological consciousness was pervading the actions of those engaged in curriculum work at that time: '[This book] is not a manual for curriculum construction since it does not describe and outline in detail the steps to be taken by a given school ... that seeks to build a curriculum' (p. 1).

Note the metaphors of *construction* and *building*. These are indicators of a technical, product centred approach to curriculum. Although Tyler disclaimed a technical interest, his work has predominated in the thinking of the majority of curriculum theorists and workers since that time. Curricula which have been constructed using Tyler's principles for guidance have generally been linear, product oriented sets of proposals and practices very much informed by a technical interest. In my view a technical interest is discernible in Tyler's work, and it is certainly discernible in the work of those who have looked to Tyler for guidance.

The technical interest is not only to be discerned by implication. It has become explicit in recent curriculum theorizing which has portrayed curriculum development as a technological exercise. At one level this is clear in the application of technology, such as computers, to the instructional process, but at another level the whole educational enterprise has been defined as a technical operation to which it is appropriate to apply the theory and practice of systems management. Rowntree (1982) is a foremost exponent and advocate of such an approach to curriculum. The technical interest is apparent in his description of education: 'Education itself can be viewed as a system — a self-adjusting combination of interacting people and things designed to accomplish some pre-determined purpose' (p. 12).

The 'pre-determined purposes' in Rowntree's model of curriculum design are contained in the objectives. It is the objectives which represent the *eideis* which will guide the process of curriculum development. These may be arrived at by taking into account the 'real' world in which the curriculum is to be implemented, but essentially the objectives are theoretical statements or principles which stand in a deterministic relationship to the world of practice. I say deterministic because it is the objectives which will determine the action in which the teacher will engage.

These pre-specified objectives will determine the design of the learning experience. The selection and organization of learning experiences will depend upon the skill of the curriculum makers. This entails the making of judgments and choices, but such decisions are strategic. They are decisions made from within a range of possible alternatives, all of which are known to produce the required results.

The product of a learning process designed in this way will be judged according to the fidelity with which the implementation of the curriculum design realizes the objectives, thus producing the desired outcome. If the 'product' of the learning experience 'measures up' to the pre-specified objectives, it will be judged 'good'. If too many of the products fail to reach the standard implicit in the objectives, the whole learning process will have to be looked at (though not necessarily the objectives themselves). Some parts of the process will have to be honed up so that the desired outcomes are obtained. The technical interest which exhibits itself in the language and practices of curriculum design has important implications for control of the curriculum.

The Technical Curriculum and Control

In the overview of the technical cognitive interest in the previous chapter, the claim was made that the technical interest was essentially an interest in the control and manipulation of the environment. It must be asked, therefore, to what extent is this true of curriculum theory informed by a technical interest and what might such a claim mean with respect to the curriculum and associated educational practices of a school.

The implicit orientation towards control of the technically informed curriculum is to be seen if we return for a moment to Rowntree. This approach to curriculum design implies that the educator will produce an educand (a pupil) who will behave according to the image (*eidos*) which we already have of a person who has learnt what we set out to teach. To accomplish this we must control both the learning environment and the learner. It is no surprise that educators talk of 'classroom management' or that educational psychologists invest their resources in attempts to discover the 'laws' which govern learning. Once discovered, the learner and/or the learning environment may be manipulated to ensure that the desired learning occurs. This is the technical interest *par excellence* in operation.

Again, let us consider the language associated with such understandings of curriculum. One of the key words is 'objectives'. The etymological association of this fundamental curriculum concept and 'objects' is interesting. The technical interest objectifies reality, that is, it regards the environment as an object. This objectified environment includes the pupils who become part of the learning environment. As objects in the learning environment their behaviour and learning are managed by the teacher. Rowntree (1982) quotes Ruskin with approval: 'Education does not mean teaching people to know what they do not know. It means teaching them to behave as they do not behave.'

So the technical interest implies certain power relationships within the learning environment. Firstly, it implies that ultimate power resides with the one or ones who formulate the objectives (that is, who control the *eidos*), for it is the *eidos* which determines what ought to occur. If we think of the example of constructing a house, the power to determine what the house will look like is vested very much with the architect. Of course, the owners who are paying to have the house constructed have an ultimate power of veto and, if things don't go according to plan, may withhold payment. This has interesting implications in the realm of curriculum with respect to the power which those who supply the finance have to control curriculum, be they governments or private interests.

The power which the expert designer exercises does not mean that the artisans have no power to control any part of the process. The trade union movement teaches us that artisans do have real powers, but they are primarily powers of reaction, not powers of action. By that I mean that artisans can facilitate, cooperate and enable or refuse, obstruct and sabotage. But all of these are the actions of receivers or agents, not those of initiators of action.

In the building process, of course, the materials which are acted upon have no power to determine their own making. Similarly, where a technical interest is at work in the learning environment the pupil will have virtually no power to determine his/her learning objectives. The learners can, however, also exercise a reactive power, by being unwilling or unable to participate in the learning environment. But again, this constitutes them as reactors, not actors in the learning situation.

Curriculum Issues

These are important problems for all those involved in the various aspects of curriculum work, be it in the design of learning experiences, in the act of teaching or in learning. For the teachers and learners, the ones either in the middle or at the end of the process, the issues are paramount, for the extent to which it is possible for them to control aspects of their own lives is at stake here. Let us, then, examine some curriculum issues in more detail. These issues will become motifs for our consideration of the curriculum implications of each of the cognitive interests. In this way the differences between the various ways of viewing and doing curriculum will become more apparent.

The Nature of the Eidos

When a technical interest informs curriculum design there is a fundamental interest in controlling the educational environment so that an educational product may result which accords with certain pre-specified objectives. Thus the more specific the objectives and the more clearly the curriculum document is set out, the better are the chances that the product will resemble that which was envisaged in the statement of objectives. Such champions of educational objectives as Gagné (1967) have argued that the specification of objectives is all that is needed in the process of curriculum construction. Once objectives are defined, everything else, even the selection of content, is determined. This insistence upon exact specification has been the inspiration for the 'teacher-proof' curriculum document: set out clearly what you want and elaborate step-by-step how you intend that the objective should be achieved, and success is guaranteed. It's as easy as making a cake!

Michael Apple has aptly illustrated this outworking of the technological consciousness in his description of the step-by-step instructions to the teacher using a set of junior school, pre-packaged science materials:

> The material specifies all of the goals. It includes everything a teacher 'needs' to teach, has the pedagogical steps a teacher must take to reach these goals already built in, and has the evaluation mechanisms built into it as well.... Not only does it pre-specify nearly all a teacher should know, say and do, but it often lays out the appropriate student responses as well. (Apple, 1980, p. 16)

This is the technically informed curriculum, directed by an *eidos* which is particular or specific and external to the act of teaching. That does not mean that the *eidos* was necessarily originally external to the teacher. In other circumstances it may well be that it is the teacher who formulates the objectives or devises the curriculum plan.

However, once the design process is completed, the plan becomes external to the planner, and has an authority which is separate from the person of the designer.

Just as the overall guiding *eidos* of the curriculum is particular, so also the objectives which direct each specific teaching act are also singular and distinctive. Indeed, the more clearly the objectives which guide the teaching act can be specified, the more predictable will be the outcome, according to this view. The debate about the nature of educational objectives (see, for instance, Stenhouse, 1975) is fundamentally a debate about the extent to which a technical cognitive interest should prevail in determining curriculum.

Responsibility and Division of Labour

It becomes clear from the preceding discussion that the technically informed curriculum implies a division of labour between the curriculum designers and the curriculum implementers. Even where teachers are involved in curriculum design, if that design process is informed by a technical cognitive interest, the roles of teacher as designer and teacher as implementer are divided.

This division of labour has interesting implications for teachers' work. Kevin Harris (1982, p.71) claims:

> Teachers are now finding themselves facing both de-skilling and devaluation of their labour power. This is most obvious in the areas of curriculum packages and technical innovations ... in many cases the existence of such packages has already de-skilled some teachers' work to the level of distributing pre-chosen material, checking pre-set tests and general filing duties.... Now there is obviously room here for vast rationalization, whereby classroom teachers could end up as not-so-glorified filing clerks while a few highly skilled experts select kits and programme the day's activities for the whole school.

The technical interest does not, however, simply mean that teachers who are de-skilled pedagogically will be left with nothing to do. It is to be remembered that the technical interest is pre-eminently an interest in control. Not only does the process of curriculum development need to be controlled, but students also need to be 'controlled' so they can achieve what the curriculum designers have planned. As teachers become de-skilled pedagogically, they become re-skilled as educational managers. The increasing emphasis upon classroom management in pre-service teacher education courses could be cited as evidence of yet another aspect of the technically informed curriculum. Apple (1982) picks up this re-emphasis which is a characteristic of the technical curriculum: 'As teachers lose control of the curricular and pedagogic skills to large publishing houses, these skills are replaced by techniques for better controlling students.'

It is interesting to speculate whether the introduction of computers into classrooms will continue to promote the ascendancy of the technical interest in curriculum. Teachers' initially low competency levels in their facility with the use of the computer may be an important factor in exacerbating the trend.

The Importance of Skill

The concept of skill is crucial, given a technical orientation to the curriculum. Preparation for teaching is regarded as teacher 'training', with the teacher education curriculum comprising the learning of a set of 'methods' by which the act of teaching will be accomplished. Micro-skills teacher training programmes are a case in point. In these teaching is portrayed as a set of sub-skills which can be learned and practised by the novice teacher. Through applying these skills in the classroom, the act of teaching is accomplished.

The 'catch 22' for the teacher in all of this, as was implied in the previous discussion of the division of labour, is that, although the accomplishment of these skills will ensure the value of the teacher's work in the society, since the teacher does not have ultimate or autonomous control in the design of the curriculum, it is open to the curriculum developers to design a curriculum which by-passes or down-plays the pedagogical skills of teachers. For instance, in the past many teachers were highly skilled in the art of teaching children to read using phonic techniques. Suddenly, or so it seemed to many of these teachers, a new method of teaching reading was being advocated: a language experience approach. No matter how sound the theoretical basis for this change of method might be, the fact remains that many teachers were de-skilled by such curriculum policy changes. They may in time have become just as expert in the new methods, but the point is that, as teachers, they did not control either the knowledge from which the change in policy followed or the policies which dictated that they change their teaching practices. In this respect, teachers do not remain immune to the technologizing and obsolescence processes at work in the technological society, any more than other trades-persons such as fitters and turners.

Curriculum Content

If we accept the proposal that it is possible for the curriculum to be informed by a technical cognitive interest, the question arises as to the content of such a curriculum. Will the technical interest only determine the form of the curriculum process or will it also determine the content?

It has been noted previously that the technical interest is an interest in control. It could thus be expected that the curriculum process will not only be concerned with controlling (or managing) the learning environment so that the desired learning can occur, but that the planned learning experiences will also be those which promote a view of knowledge as sets of rules and procedures or unquestionable 'truths'. Knowledge is regarded as a commodity, a means to an end: 'Our task is ... to get him [sic, i.e. the learner] to his objectives' (Rowntree, 1982). This is what Giroux (1981) calls the 'culture of positivism':

> In this view, knowledge is objective, 'bounded' and 'out there'. Classroom knowledge is often treated as an external body of information, the production of which appears to be independent of human beings. From this perspective, human knowledge is viewed as being independent of time and place; it becomes universalized ahistorical knowledge. Moreover it is expressed in a language which is basically technical and allegedly value free.... Knowledge, then, becomes not only countable and measurable, it also becomes impersonal. Teaching in this pedagogical paradigm is usually discipline-based and treats subject matter in a compartmentalized and atomized fashion. (pp. 52–3)

The question of the content of the curriculum is a vexed one for those engaged in curriculum development. Philosophers of education such as Paul Hirst and R.S. Peters (1970) have argued on logical grounds that curriculum content should be formed around the concept of 'worthwhile activities', and that these worthwhile activities can be identified and categorized into certain 'forms of knowlege'.

The work of Hirst and Peters has been highly influential in legitimating the content and organization of the academically oriented hegemonic curriculum (Connell *et al.*, 1982) in both Britain and Australia. Yet the representation of knowledge as being divisible into a set of separate and immutable categories is just the sort of ahistorical, objectivist thinking which Giroux criticizes. Hirst and Peters claim that 'within the domain of objective experience and knowledge, there are such radical differences of kind that ... [achievements] in one domain must be recognized as radically different from those in any other' (p. 65). Here there is no acknowledgment that knowledge is socially constructed or that our constructions have historical and temporal antecedents which give a unity to all human knowledge and experience.

Once the basis for the organization of knowledge in the curriculum has been established, the specific content of the various areas of knowledge needs to be decided. (That order of dealing with the question assumes that curriculum practice occurs in the order that curriculum theory describes. For the sake of the argument we will proceed as if such were the case.) It is in the subject matter which is selected for instruction and the manner of that instruction that the technical interest is also clearly discernible. The technically informed curriculum is not only bound by the culture of positivism as far as the selection of content is concerned, but the methodology by which the content is imparted is also determined by positivistic requirements about objectivity and outcomes. Thus, teachers who might want to allow students to express their scientific understandings by writing in descriptive or poetic ways are constrained by the knowledge that Higher School Certificate examiners want 'facts' expressed in precise, non-emotive language. This is not to claim that such precision is unimportant, but merely to regret an orientation to learning which strictly constructs knowledge according to means–end criteria, thus thwarting much of the potential richness in the students' understandings of the world. More importantly, it is to regret an orientation towards knowledge which uses learning to preserve and reproduce the established power relationships of schooling. (These notions of how the technical interest may act to thwart understanding and autonomy will be taken up in later chapters when we consider the practical and the emancipatory interests.)

The Meaning of Evaluation

Evaluation has become an important element in the curriculum field. This has happened partly as a consequence of a demand by the financiers of public education for some accountability on the part of those engaged in the educational enterprise, and also from educators themselves, who have become aware of the need to justify and legitimate their practices. The latter source of motivation towards evaluation is often related in unrecognized ways to the former.

Curriculum evaluation, however, is often portrayed as having nothing to do with 'outside' influences, but only to do with the curriculum process itself. We need only to hark back to Tyler (1949) or to consider the more recent curriculum model of Rowntree (1982) to see how the practice of evaluation is portrayed as being part of the curriculum process rather than having other purposes. Although evaluation is represented as being part of the process of curriculum development, in these technically informed linear models of curriculum development evaluation is nevertheless separate from the teaching process, just as the design of the curriculum is also separate from the act of teaching/learning. Since this is the case, evaluation, like curriculum design, can in principle and in practice be undertaken and controlled by those other than the teacher or learners. So, although the inclusion of evaluation provisions in these models of curriculum development appears quite rational, the underlying value of a technically informed evaluation exercise will be of control.

When considering evaluation we are never free of politics in the macro sense of government and in the micro-political sense of who has the power in the *polis* to determine what education shall comprise. Often, however, when a curriculum is informed by a technical interest the political nature of evaluation and the interest in control are disguised. The making of evaluative judgments is presented as an objective, value-free enterprise.

The important principle underlying the process of evaluation within a technically informed curriculum is the need to make an assessment of how closely the product matches the guiding *eidos*. It is the product which is evaluated, and the evaluation, to be authoritative and legitimate, should take the form of measurement. The process of evaluation in a curriculum informed by a technical interest is conceptually no different from the evaluation of the success of enterprises in the physical world. Lawton (1980) identifies two models of evaluation in the physical world which have been taken up and applied to educational evaluation: The Classical (or agricultural-botanical) Research Model and The Research and Development (or industrial, factory) Model. These models are closely related and involve essentially making assessments of the success of an operation by evaluating the changes which have occurred in the objects which have been the focus of attention. Lawton (1980, p. 112) explains the classical experimental approach to evaluation:

> The classical experimental approach to evaluation treats the problem of evaluating the success of any particular learning programme, or curriculum project or new text book as a simple matter, essentially the same as an experiment in agriculture or botany. An educationist measures success just as an agriculturalist might test the efficiency of a new fertilizer by: (i) measuring the height of a plant; (ii) applying the fertilizer for a given amount of time; then (iii) measuring again, comparing the height of the 'experimental' plants with that of plants in a control group.

The industrial model is similar, except that evaluation is regarded as being 'more like the industrial process of improving upon or testing out a product.'

In each of these approaches to curriculum evaluation there is evidence of technical reasoning. The learners are objectified and learning is regarded as a product which can be evaluated against predetermined criteria or against other products which have been produced under different circumstances. There are severe problems associated with this objectifying approach to curriculum evaluation. Many of these are measurement problems; for example, the act of measuring the growth of a plant may not affect the plant, while the act of testing the learner is itself likely to become part of the learning act. Measurement specialists recognize and react to such problems by working to refine measurement procedures. But more fundamental assumptions are at stake here. The notion that atomistic pieces of learning can be identified and measured is an assumption which trivializes the teaching-learning act. Education consists of more than a list of separate pieces of knowledge or behaviours which can be identified and measured.

Yet despite such objections and problems, some curriculum theorists continue to talk as if evaluation is a matter of comparing an outcome with some preconceived *eidos*. Marsh and Stafford (1984), for example, advocate the use of norm-referenced testing for evaluation purposes, but admit: 'It would be easier if teachers were able to use absolute measures with their teaching just as scientists can use exact standards for elements, metals, units of length, area and volume.' An underlying technical interest is discernible here, even though it is admitted that such precision of measurement is not totally applicable to education. The implication of such thinking is that if only we could refine the measures and, perhaps, if only pupils would act a little more like inanimate objects to which we could apply our measuring instruments, then education could operate as empirical-analytic science.

If such technically informed evaluation procedures objectify the learner, they also serve to reinforce the idea that the act of teaching is a mechanistic one, in Lawton's terms analogous to a 'treatment' applied to some objects. The teacher similarly is constituted as the one who does the applying. If the product does not 'measure up', then either the treatment or the application thereof must be improved. Although such an orientation to educational evaluation and improvement has appeal in its simplicity and scientific portrayal, it has the problem of removing control of the teaching/learning process from the teachers and learners. Power both to determine and to judge what teachers and learners must do is vested elsewhere.

Drawing Together

In the discussion of curriculum in this chapter, a macro-view of the process of curriculum making has been largely taken. That is, curriculum development has been discussed as if it were a large-scale enterprise, as indeed much curriculum development at a system, region and sometimes even school level is. However, it must always be remembered that the curriculum is developed even as it is implemented through the 'making' actions of the teachers. It is important to recognize that the technical interest can operate at the level of the classroom as well as in the closets of the curriculum designers and evaluators.

The technical interest has important consequences for the classroom practitioner. If the curriculum is designed elsewhere, the teacher will be under pressure to be productive in the ways envisaged by the designers (which, as we have seen, is really reproductive work). The quality of the teacher's work will then be judged by the products of his/her actions. This has implications for the nature and status of teachers' work.

It is possible and, given the hegemony of the technological consciousness within Western societies, probable that a teacher's own perception of the nature of the educational enterprise as it is enacted in the classroom will also be informed by a technical interest. What this means for the teacher who takes seriously the task of curriculum development in relation to his/her own classroom, but whose endeavours to be engaged in curriculum development are informed by a technical interest, we will investigate in the following chapter.

Chapter 3

Teachers as Curriculum Makers

Much has been implied in the theoretical explorations of the previous chapter about the work of teachers. The task of this chapter is to provide a basis upon which the authenticity of these theorems about the nature and construction of teachers' curriculum work can be judged. This task will be pursued through a consideration of the practices of those engaged in the everyday reality of classroom life. To do that it is necessary to explore what the previous analysis means in the light of curriculum practice. That is, it is the theorems which are to be scrutinized in the light of the practice of teachers, not practice in the light of the theory. Thus, the present task is to identify, if possible, evidence of a technical interest in curriculum practices. This is to be done, not to make judgments about those practices, but to judge the authenticity of the theoretical construct of the technical cognitive interest in relation to curriculum practice.

One way of proceeding would be to take a macro-view of the curriculum and make some judgments about whether it is possible to discern a technical interest in the curriculum of schools at large. Such across-sites analyses have been conducted previously in a number of places. Mention was made above of Apple's (1980) description of the technically informed junior science curriculum in which both content and method of imparting were carefully laid out for the teacher. Anyon (1979) and Giroux (1981) have both explored in different ways how the technological consciousness, as it is worked out through the culture of positivism, influences the way in which history is conceived and taught in American schools. What seems more appropriate in this present work is to explore the outworking of the technical interest at the level of the classroom.

Traditional curriculum theory separates curriculum processes into design, dissemination, implementation, evaluation and perhaps in-

novation. For all of these curriculum processes, apart from implementation (and perhaps evaluation) the association with classrooms is
at best tentative. Important aspects of curriculum development are
portrayed as taking place away from the sites of classroom practice,
and only penetrating such sites as fully formed prescriptions to be put
into effect at the chalk-face. (Again, the etymological association
between the term 'implementation' and the technical term 'implement'
is interesting to contemplate.) But there is a very real sense in which
curriculum development takes place at the level of classroom practice,
despite what might have been designed elsewhere. This is, of course,
why so-called curriculum developers often tear their hair in despair.
All their careful work of designing a curriculum can come to naught
unless the classroom operators can be persuaded to adopt their recommendations. Classroom teachers, however, invariably adapt curriculum recommendations, hence the need, in the minds of technically
informed curriculum developers, for the teacher-proof curriculum.
Ultimately, however, the curriculum is that which students experience in the learning environment. No matter how sophisticated the
plans might be, it is through the transactions of the classroom that the
real curriculum is developed. So it is to the classroom practitioners
that we shall turn here to seek evidence of the technical interest.

All of the teachers whose work will be described below were
engaged in projects aimed at systematically developing and improving
their classroom curriculum practices. Most of these were action research projects which involved the practitioners taking deliberate,
strategic action to change some aspect of their practice or to incorporate some 'new' idea into their classroom. These are teachers who
take seriously the task of curriculum development at the classroom
level.

The sources of information about these teachers' classroom curriculum practices were mainly accounts of the curriculum developments
written by the teachers themselves, supplemented in some cases by
interviews. The focus here will be, not so much upon what the
teachers actually did in the course of the curriculum development
(although short accounts of the projects in which they participated
will be given), as upon an analysis of the sort of knowledge that was
created out of the project for the practitioners, and the kinds of actions
in which they engaged as part of the development. For it is in these
two aspects of the teachers' work that the technical interest will
manifest itself.

It has been argued above that the technical interest is essentially
product-centred. This means that if a technical interest informs a

teacher's work we would expect to see a concern with the products of the development. Attempts to develop the curriculum in such a teacher's classroom would be characterized by the application of standards of excellence to the work produced as a consequence of the development. The production of acceptable educational products is dependent upon the development of skills in both pupil and teacher. Classroom curriculum development, therefore, will be utilized as a means of honing teaching skills and implementing ideas which will improve the work output of the students.

Where a teacher's work in a curriculum development project was informed by a technical interest, that interest would constitute the knowledge generated for the teacher through the project as 'know-how' or 'know-what' knowledge; that is, knowledge about *how* best to go about doing things and of *what* it might be best to go about doing. Such knowledge will result in efficient and effective productive (making) action.

Project Profiles

It must be stressed that for the most part the initiators of these projects did not conceive or plan them specifically as technical projects. In fact the projects were mostly undertaken as a consequence of aspirations for improved classroom practices arising from a practical interest in understanding and meaning-making. So pervasive is the technical interest in production and control, however, that in all of these projects it is possible to identify teachers whose work was informed by a technical interest. Profiles of the projects are given here, but these projects will also be referred to in subsequent chapters. I have chosen the projects for consideration from a range of Australian states.

The Karrivale Project

The Karrivale project was structurally classified as an in-service course. It was initiated by a group of high school teachers who wanted to put into practice the investigative and reflective recommendations of the Martin Report into English Teaching in Western Australian schools. This report advocated a meaning-making approach to English teaching. It stressed the importance of a writing process which reflected the way in which writers actually work, placing importance upon such aspects as drafting and a concern with audience. Reading processes were also portrayed as meaning-making experiences rather than de-coding exercises. Group work and the use of learning journals were classroom practices supported by the Report as being consistent with its principles of meaning-making.

In essence, the Martin Report can be judged as being informed by a practical interest in the establishment of meaningful experiences for English students. The concerns of the teachers who initiated the Karrivale project were that, although the Report had been hailed in the Education Department, there was little evidence of the penetration of its recommendations to the level of the classroom. The project was thus conceived as one which would examine the theories upon which the Report was grounded and attempt to explore the application of these theories to practice.

The project was organizationally situated at Karrivale High School and involved twenty-four teachers from eleven schools. The participants were divided into three strands. Strand A consisted of four teachers who organized and administered the project. These teachers facilitated the reflection sessions for the other teachers and opened their classrooms to the Strand B teachers for observation. Strand B was a group of less experienced teachers who participated or observed in the Strand A teachers' classrooms on three afternoons a term, meeting for two hours after school to discuss and reflect upon their experiences. They then experimented in their own classes with the ideas they were considering. Strand C was a group of more experienced teachers who met on alternative afternoons to the Strand B teachers. These teachers reflected collaboratively upon projects they were undertaking in their own classrooms to implement some of the principles of the Report. All teachers who participated in the project undertook to write about their own classroom experiments and reflections.

Although the project overall was concerned with meaning-making, some of the participating teachers' work provides evidence of a technical interest, and it is the work of these teachers which will be of concern here. We will return to the work of some of the other teachers in later chapters.

Change in Small Schools

This was a large curriculum development project in which 213 primary school principals investigated ways of initiating some aspect of curriculum change in their schools. The action research process was the medium through which change was to be effected in the schools. The principals came together in workshop sessions to learn about the pinciples of action research, and then returned to their schools to initiate changes using the methodology.

This project had many characteristics of a 'top-down' model of innovation and implementation of change. As such it incorporates many characteristics consistent with a technical knowledge-constitutive interest. This interest is evidenced by the following features of the project: the 'idea' for the project came from elsewhere, it was not generated by the principals themselves; participants consented to being involved in the project without being necessarily personally committed to the ideas which guided its development; the skill of the organizers in instructing the participants in the change process was crucial to its success; the outcome was end-directed rather than practice-centred, that is, the success of a principal's project was determined by whether the predetermined changes were implemented, rather than on the basis of a professional judgment about the meaning or value of the change. This is not to suggest that nothing of value resulted from the project. Many of the principals' reports acknowledge valuable changes both in their relationships with staff and in the curriculum practices of their schools.

The Language Development Project

The Australian National Language Development Project, initiated by the Curriculum Development Centre in 1976, aimed to foster the development of listening, speaking, reading and writing in children in school years 5–8. The investigations into these areas were to proceed through cooperative curriculum development which incorporated teachers as participants in the projects and in the development and production of curriculum materials.

The project was taken up in each state and territory of the Commonwealth, each focusing on a different aspect of language. The South Australian project focused upon writing. Thirty teachers from ten schools, state and private, formed a teacher network. The project was facilitated by a full-time coordinator and a task-force of educational officers and advisors.

The project had three phases. During the first phase the investigative groups were formed and the participating teachers retrospectively documented their classroom practices. During the next phase teachers undertook individual action research curriculum development projects in their own classrooms. The final phase of the project saw teachers engaging in collaborative development projects. They also documented their experiences by writing accounts of their projects for sharing with other teachers.

Investigating Language and Learning

At Waterford High School in Tasmania, Australia, a team of teachers responsible for teaching year 8 classes was invited to undertake an investigative project as part of the national Language and Learning Project. Some members of the team had reservations but were obliged to participate because of the decision that a whole year team should be involved.

The staff was released for four days during the year to meet for discussion, planning and reflection. Three cycles of action and reflection are discernible in the documented life of the project. The first cycle began with reflection. A period of reading and informal discussion was followed by a two-day workshop during which teachers were introduced to a theoretical model of language and a range of language activities. These were subsequently trialled in the teachers' classes. These early experiences were shared at another whole-day workshop early in second term. Discussion at the workshop focused on how language activities offered to students could be coordinated across all classes. A monitoring system was devised by the teachers. Back in their classes the teachers trialled language activities which they had devised for their classes and monitored the effectiveness of these by such means as recording student discussion groups, analyzing student's writing in all subjects and constructing a profile of language activities engaged in by one class over a three-week period. A final day's review conference was held at the end of the year for teachers to reflect upon and document their experiences.

Investigating Learning in Your Classroom

The organizers of this project believed that teacher development through in-service education needs to be classroom-based if it is to meet the professional needs of teachers in real ways. So this project began as a two-day in-service course during which the participants reflected upon learning and planned strategies for monitoring and improving the learning occurring in their classrooms. The participating teachers were from all sectors of the schooling system. The focus of the project was upon the ways in which teachers articulate and build their own theoretical and practical learning about children, classrooms and content. Following the initial conference, the group continued to meet to reflect upon their classroom-based projects. There was a strong emphasis in the project upon creating data which would provide evidence of both the teachers' and the pupils' learning which was occurring as a consequence of the teachers' actions and reflections. Teachers kept checklists, portfolios and files of work, logs and diaries and used interviews, questionnaires, audio and video tapes, and still photography to document and analyze the learning.

Looking into the Projects

Since the technical interest is a knowledge-constitutive interest, we will look for evidence of a technical interest by considering initially the knowledge which was generated for and by some of the participants through involvement in these curriculum projects. Specifically, we will consider the nature of the knowledge which was generated, the value which the practitioners ascribed to 'theoretical' knowledge, and the theory/practice relationship. At the 'output' end of the technical theory/practice relationship, we will consider the actions in which the practitioners engaged by considering the focus, the outcome and the quality of their actions.

Knowledge Generated

The technical interest is an interest in control. Therefore, if such an interest does inform the knowledge and work of teachers engaged in curriculum development in their classrooms, among other things we would expect that an important aspect of their endeavours would be gaining control over their teaching situation so that they can produce what they set out to produce. In turn, what follows from this interest is that the sort of knowledge which teachers, whose work is informed by a technical cognitive interest, gain from involvement in a curriculum development project is knowledge of how to do things better. Thus, the knowledge generated is 'skill knowledge': knowledge of how to act in certain situations to improve the outcome of the act of teaching.

In the Karrivale project some of the participants spent time observing other teachers' classes. This was regarded as valuable because it provided both ideas about what one might do and examples of practices against which the teachers might judge their own actions. One of the teachers, Pamela, commented in an interview upon the value of these observational times:

> I'd think: well he hasn't really raised his voice ... he's handled that really well, I would have done it this way (which has usually ended up in disaster).... And even the little things like: the teachers would often talk to their kids before [they] came into the classroom ... I'd think 'well how often do I actually do that?'

A comment by one of the other teachers who had been involved in the classroom observation sessions also reflects the concern for the development of skill knowledge:

> Being able to watch the fact that the kids do talk made me better able to judge what my kids did in groups. I think I can now walk along and tell when they're just chattering or when actually talking on task; and that's something ... I wasn't able to do.

One of the features of technical knowledge is that it tends to be situation-specific; each situation requires its own set of rules or principles for action. Two of the teachers in the Karrivale project made comments which suggested that the knowledge which they had gained through participation in the project was of this specific kind.

Una had conducted a project with her year 8 class which introduced them to a writing process involving drafting, editing and publishing their work. The following year she found that the same principles could not easily be transferred to a year 10 class:

> I had year ten's this year.... I think by the time kids are in year ten we have already very strongly reinforced their ideas about how they ought to be going about things and I wasn't about to change that much at all. I've got a very simplified way of carrying through some of the Karrivale ideas. I really look forward next year to starting from scratch with a group of year eight students.

Notice here that the teacher's perceived inability to change an aspect of her curriculum stems from the inculcation into the students of technological principles of learning; that there is a set procedure to follow. If that procedure has been shown to be successful, there is real resistance to the introduction of alternative ways of acting. Thus it is not only the teachers who find difficulty in adapting ideas from one situation to the next, their problems are multiplied by the attitudes of their students.

Another teacher, Hannah, commented upon the difficulty of applying ideas from one situation to another:

> The year eight programme that [the Karrivale teachers] worked out last year, I've virtually used for term one and so did the other year eight teachers.... But ... it didn't work for everyone. It's hard just taking someone else's programme and saying — right, it's worked for them, it's going to work for me, because it doesn't.

What is implied here is a form of technical adaptation. Like dress patterns, programmes may fit perfectly in one case, but need alteration when applied to another situation.

Theory

The technical interest, which generates rule-following action designed to achieve pre-specified objectives, will be represented by two separate but compatible attitudes to 'theory' on the part of practitioners. Theoretical statements are regarded as being either 'abstract' or 'practical'. Abstract theories are thought of as being developed in isolation from and having no relevance to practice. Practical theory is, on the other hand, regarded as being authoritative, providing the practitioner with sets of directives to be applied in the classroom.

The attitude that theory and practice have little to do with one another is often expressed by teachers in similar ways to this comment by Hannah: 'To me still, theory is there and to me the important thing is the practicalities of the classroom and, even now, I guess they should blend in nicely, but they somehow don't.' Nevertheless, written documents such as the Martin Report, which provided the theoretical focus for the Karrivale project, were regarded as being important by this group of teachers. Such theoretical statements are regarded as being 'practical' because they provide sources of justification for actions and ideas which will promote quality products: 'Using the model "The Writing Process" and sharing the theory with them, does help students to produce better quality work, not just a reproduced piece with surface errors corrected.'

Curriculum development processes may also be regarded as 'practical theories'. We shall see later (in chapter 8) that action research is a process which centrally engages practitioners in improving aspects of educational practice. Action research is increasingly being utilized for school-based curriculum development. Sometimes, however, its utilization indicates a technical interest; that is, it is believed that the application of the methodology will guarantee worthwhile curriculum outcomes. This technological approach to using action research as a curriculum development process is reflected in the following school principal's comment from the Change in Small Schools Project. The Principal was describing his initial introduction of the action research process to the staff of his school:

> An outline of the steps to be undertaken in action research planning and its advantages for both classroom use and staff decisions was given.... It was pointed out that the plan needed to be followed in some detail initially.

This is an instance of practical theory. The action research process becomes a prescription for action. It must be followed step-by-step so that an acceptable outcome might be produced.

Teachers are often denigrated for having scant regard for theory, yet the technological consciousness which places theory in an authoritative, hierarchical relationship with practice has so often left teachers feeling betrayed. This sentiment was implicit in the comment of another of the Karrivale teachers:

> When I saw them putting it into practice [the theory] became important to me; but initially I was frightened that it was going to be all theory and no practice.... I always tend to be a little bit cynical, or had been in the past, with a lot of theories that didn't seem to work very well in the classroom.

Note here also the implication that theory comes from elsewhere, and is 'put into practice' by the 'artisans' in the teaching situation. What is respected is the type of 'theory' which can be applied directly to the practical situation. This leads us into a consideration of the theory/practice relationship.

Theory/Practice

Teachers often acknowledged the applicability of theory of their practical situation where the theory confirmed already existing knowledge regarding practice. Theory directs, confirms and legitimizes practice. This is evident in a comment made by Glenda regarding the theory with which she had come in contact during a whole-school curriculum development: 'The outside theories were really reinforcing what I was doing, so it was more a case of feeling that you weren't alone, that other people had tried it.' In this way, Glenda appeared to personalize the theoretical principles which accorded with those changes she was attempting to implement in her classes.

An interesting example of a teacher 'taking over' a theoretically justified practice is the account that Hansen, one of the South Australian Language and Learning teachers, gives of her adoption of group work when she returned to teaching after a period of 'motherhood' absence. She describes the difficulties of adopting new educational ideas after a decade of absence from the classroom. After she, and presumably other teachers had 'given groups a go' she perceived 'acceptance of Group Work by the school community' in part because of 'proven achievement in basic skills'. She then discusses 'ten easy steps' that a teacher 'groping into groups' might take.

Hansen gives an inspirational and sympathetic account of the implementation of group work so that one is attracted to the stimulating learning environment being provided for the children. Furthermore she is committed to the concept of group work to the extent of making the theory her own; 'still committed to Group Work', she reports. Yet the interest is technical. Throughout her report, for instance, she capitalizes the term 'Group Work'. The capitals perhaps suggest that group work is an *eidos* to be implemented rather than a practice to be incorporated into one's repertoire of classroom actions. Again, groups are engaged because of their 'proven achievement in basic skills'. This is evidence of a product orientation towards the incorporation of various practices into her teaching repertoire.

A more obvious example of this personalization of 'good' theory which is indicative of a technical interest is provided by the Waterford Language and Learning project. The theoretical model which informed this project was developed by the National Working Party on the Role of Language in Learning (Curriculum Development Centre, 1980). The technical way in which this theory was adopted by some of the teachers is discernible in this statement by one of the teachers originally coopted into the project:

> Because of the pressures that exist while working in this school, I was very reluctant to enter this project ... [but] when

the ideas and expectations behind the project became apparent,
I became far more enthusiastic.... I used the language activities
as a natural accompaniment to my normal practical programme ... the results were effective and the creative results
were very rewarding.

Identifying this as a technical relationship of theory to practice is not
to deny the worthwhileness of the teacher's work with her class.
Rather it is to highlight the technical control which she had of her
knowledge and action. This contrasts with a science teacher's comment which reveals a theory/practice relationship, not entirely
governed by the effectiveness of outcomes, but centred in the value of
the learning environment: 'The success of the project for me has been
the change in me. I now look for opportunities to use language more
in my attempt to provide a good language environment for my
students.'

The difference here is subtle, but crucial. It is the difference
between the technical and the practical knowledge-constitutive interest. The practitioner whose knowledge is constituted by a technical
interest perceives the external *eidos* as a finite plan, and uses his/her
skills to modify, adapt and apply it in a different situation to produce
an outcome that is judged in terms of efficiency and effectiveness. On
the other hand, the practitioner whose work is informed by a practical
interest grasps the *eidos* in terms of principles, relying upon practical
judgment as a basis for decisions. What is important for him/her is
understanding and the creation of a meaningful learning environment.

Action Focus

Being involved in these projects was clearly important for some
teachers because the group meetings provided a source of ideas which
could then be tried out in the participant's classroom. Some of the
teachers in the Karrivale project found the observational times in other
teachers' classes the most valuable aspect of the project because they
gave them ideas which they could try out in their own classes. The
reproductive actions of teachers whose work is informed by a technical interest are reflected in this comment by Anne: 'I'm still using
ideas.... They [one of the project teachers] had "how to write a
business letter" and "how to write a personal letter" — they had them
mounted on card in their room — I've done that in my room....'

In the written account of her personal project, Una relates that
she imparted writing strategies to her students by having them 'com-

plete [an] activity by following a highly prescriptive procedure detailed on a written hand-out "The Writing Process".' In this case 'The Writing Process' has taken the form of an external *eidos* to be implemented through the mediation of the teacher's and the pupils' *techne* (skills). Through the skilled implementation of this procedure written pieces of work are produced. The action of implementing the procedure, as well as the actions of the students in producing their pieces of work, is a form of *poietike*, technical (making) action.

When action research is employed in the process of curriculum development for the dissemination of particular ideas rather than as a reflective process, it operates in the technical mode. Engaging in action research (or any process of curriculum development) in a technical mode leaves open the possibility that participants may be coopted into working in pseudo-collaborative ways to achieve ends which have been determined prior to the initiation of the project. An example of this is to be found in a report by a principal involved in the Change in Small Schools Project:

> Whilst I do not want absolute uniformity in the classroom, there are elements in each room which would be desirable in all the rooms if only I can find a way to encourage those with the ideas to be aware that the ideas are worthwhile and beneficial if shared.

The technical interest in this way of working is evidenced by the manner in which 'ideas' are regarded as 'entities' to be reproduced from one site to another. The technical mode of work is further indicated by the overseer role adopted by the principal. This interest became even more evident with the visit to the school of the next level of overseer:

> Inspector visited. Thought our handwriting needed improvement which was not news to the principal. This was providential because it gave focus to the next staff meeting where teachers decided on a new plan of action, viz. Principal to observe all teachers taking a lesson on handwriting and share findings.

Note the technical features here: the authority figures of the inspector and principal have access to the true *eidos* of what constitutes good handwriting, and it is the principal who will judge the effectiveness of the teachers' actions and mediate the results. Skill, not practitioner judgment, is an important factor as is teacher attitude towards the product, not towards their practice. Later in the report the writer noted: 'Handwriting is improving, as is teacher attitude towards neatness in all written work.'

A predominant concern with the final product is reflected in the comments of a number of other teachers who participated in these various projects. In interview Hannah, one of the teachers in the Karrivale project, described her interest in achieving a desirable product and her observation of another teacher which she believed would assist her to this end: 'The work that M. gets from those kids is just excellent and I really wanted to see what she did and how she got that final product.' In her written account she recognizes that perhaps the product is not the whole story: 'A faultless, imaginative piece of writing is wonderful but should the emphasis and reward come from the final product only?' But this insight is not developed and effective approaches remain the focus both in her written report of the project she undertook and in her later verbal descriptions of that work.

Target of Action

The focus of action in technically informed curriculum projects is the implementation of ideas. More specifically, however, ideas are implemented so that the products of the educational process can be improved. The success of a project is judged in terms of the tangible products, that is, the pieces of work produced by the pupils as a consequence of the development process.

In an interview Anne justified her judgment of the success of her actions by reference to the quality of the product: 'It's been successful — the work produced has been quite outstanding.' Later, commenting upon the success of implementing a shared writing idea in her class, she explained: 'When I read it to the other teachers, they couldn't get over it; these two weak little boys, this is what they had produced. That really worked.' Clearly the product is that by which the achievement of a goal is measured. Again, for Una the success of the implementation of the writing strategies mentioned above was judged by the products: 'Certainly, in terms of the quality of their work output; it really was a tremendous difference. It was quite remarkable, the standard of some of the work.'

As was pointed out in the theoretical investigation in the previous chapter of the implications of a technical interest for curriculum development, measurement provides the basis upon which improvement is judged to have occurred. It would follow that a technical interest would reflect a concern to be able to document the amount of improvement which had taken place as a consequence of the curriculum development being undertaken. This concern is evident in this statement by one of the principals in the Change in Small Schools Project: 'General idea: improvement in the teaching and publication of writing.... A benchmark sample is to be kept and new work undertaken as a result of this action step will be judged against that sample.' Improvement is regarded to a certain extent as unproblematic here: as being readily perceivable, if not measurable, in the products of the actions.

It has previously been argued that fundamentally the technical interest is an interest in control. We need to ask, then, if the theory of the technical interest is to have any authenticity in the realm of classroom practice, whether there was an interest in control evident in the work of these teachers. There is evidence of a concern with control in many of the comments cited previously. For instance, it was the principal who was to observe the various handwriting lessons and 'share findings'. Why, it might be asked, did he/she not relieve teachers of their classes for short periods to allow them to observe each other's lessons? One senses a concern to oversee and control the sharing of ideas. We can recall Una's written handout on 'The Writing Process'. Here the process, which is theoretically a liberating one, is controlled and made manageable for both teacher and pupil. Production of 'good' work is made dependent upon following a set procedure. We noted also Patty's statement about being able, as a consequence of engaging in the project, to tell when her students were 'just chattering' and when they were 'on task'. Skills of control were clearly important here.

The technical interest would also make the task of controlling the actual process of curriculum development an important one for the initiator of the development project. We recall in this regard the principal who outlined the action research steps to his/her staff, pointing out that 'the plan needed to be followed in some detail initially'. He/she exhibits evidence of just such an interest in controlling the process of development by drawing attention to a set of procedures which must be carefully followed for the project to succeed.

Quality of Action

It is clear from the foregoing analysis of action in the technical mode that the qualities by which the practitioners would want their actions to be judged are those of efficiency and effectiveness.

Anne expressed her confidence in the improved quality of her own and her pupils' work and the consequent lessening of her concern for quantity: 'If I ever felt that somebody may say there's not sufficient pieces produced, then I feel I'm confident enough to justify what I've done.' Paul, a teacher involved in the Investigating Learning in Your Classroom Project, was dissatisfied with the effectiveness of his teaching due partly to his own inefficiency: 'The problem is that I've got some undefined idealistic notion of what [teaching] means and I suppose the difficulty is that I can't live up to the ideal because of my own organizational limitations.' Becoming involved in an action research curriculum development project, however, provided him with 'a practical means of trying to achieve goals that I held in principle.' Una at no time questioned the effectiveness of her own practice, but valued efficiency in the work of her pupils: 'Over time, the students' increased familiarity with the various steps in the writing process has made them more efficient writers.'

Many of the principals who participated in the Change in Small Schools Project indicated that they valued efficiency and effectiveness as the qualities promoted by their projects. One principal reported a focus upon time management for his/her project. Another principal's comment reflects a concern with efficiency: 'Discussion led to a consensus of opinion that the school could develop sequential programs in key areas of the curriculum, and such programs [would] be quite prescriptive and binding on all staff of the school.' This prescription was intended to promote efficiency in the teaching programme of the school: 'Some teachers ... were using inefficient processes, and showed obvious enthusiasm for the processes brought to their attention.' Note in these comments also the implicit interest in control. Programmes were to be 'quite prescriptive and binding' on all staff.

In Summary

In our theoretical investigation of the technical interest, a number of factors were identified as being the constitutive elements of knowledge and action informed by this interest. These factors flowed from an interest in controlling the environment. Control is important to ensure that existing conditions are reproduced and, hence, that the continued survival of both the species itself and the various forms of social and cultural life which have been developed to sustain that existence are also maintained. Since education is, and has always been, an integral part of the survival and maintenance process, we would expect that educational practices would also be subject to technical interests. In most societies schools are the cultural structures through which education is promulgated, so we would further expect that the technical interest would also manifest itself in the curriculum of schools.

In this chapter we have sought evidence of the technical interest in the curriculum development practices of teachers. It was proposed that evidence would be provided through an examination of the knowledge which teachers generated by engaging in curriculum development projects and the actions which they took as a consequence of engaging in such work. Such evidence has been identifiable in the written and verbal accounts of the teachers' work examined in this chapter.

The technical interest manifests itself in knowledge which is essentially ideas oriented. 'Theory' is valued to the extent that it is 'practical', that is, directly applicable to practice without the necessity to be reinterpreted. Theory has a prescriptive, not a propositional relationship to practice when work is informed by a technical interest. Action is, then, product related. As well as being guided by prescriptive ideas, action informed by a technical interest is subject to supervision by others. Furthermore, the products of action are judged according to the way in which they measure up to prescribed criteria.

It is not the case that every one of the reports examined above provided evidence of all of these constitutive elements. What is more important is that across a range of reports of the curriculum work of a number of teachers, these indicators of the technical interest are discernible. An examination of the work of teachers, therefore, does provide a basis for regarding Habermas' theorems concerning the constitutive nature of the technical interest as authentic.

Chapter 4

Curriculum as Practice

For our previous exploration of the various aspects of the technical interest with respect to human action, I took as a starting point the writings of Aristotle. In this chapter we will consider the practical interest in some more detail, and as this interest constitutes both a form of knowing and of acting also considered by Aristotle, we shall return again to the writings of that ancient sage rather than pursuing the argument through the reconstructive discourse of Habermas. The form of action with which we shall be concerned here is that which Aristotle identifies and analyzes as being dependent upon human judgments. These are judgments which are made on the basis of an interpretation of the meaning of a situation by those responsible for taking the action.

Making meaning through an act of interpretation, and thus providing a basis for making decisions about action, is known as hermeneutical interpretation. Hermeneutics is a form of knowledge associated most often with scriptural interpretation in theological studies. It was (and is) considered important by the theologically inclined to be able to provide a meaningful interpretation of Scripture in order to discern guidance for future action. Hermeneutics has not remained the preserve of theologians, however. Some modern (particularly European) philosophers, for example, Heidegger, Gadamer (1977), and Ricoeur (1979), have argued that hermeneutical interpretation should be reinstated as a fundamental form of knowledge for modern society. It is argued that hermeneutical understanding is a pre-eminent form of knowledge upon which action can proceed. Rather than simply claiming that the knowledge and application of sets of rules is a sufficient basis for action, hermeneutics reminds us of the importance of making decisions about both the meaning of the rules and the situation in which they are to be applied before action is taken.

The philosophers mentioned above have all returned in varying ways to the works of Aristotle for an understanding of what action based upon interpretative judgments might imply. The action with which they (and we) are concerned in this context is action that recognizes and respects the part played by human reason in the act of decision-making. We have noted before that Habermas contends that the reinstatement of the primacy of human reason as a basis for action (as against rule-following) can be argued from 'first principles'. He argues that it is possible to distil these principles from a reconstruction of the evolution of the human species rather than by reference to Aristotle (see chapter 2). But the practical interest is aptly treated in the Aristotelian work, which again provides some shortcuts to an understanding of the Habermasian concepts. We shall, thus, step aside for a moment from education and curriculum concerns and delve into ancient Greek politics and language. Having made this excursis, the implications which these forms of knowledge and action have for education will become evident.

Aristotle and the Practical Interest

The first question which must be addressed here is the meaning of 'practical' in this context. For the Athenian Greeks the practical life was the political life; that is, the life which involved the realm of interaction with other men ('men' is used deliberately here, since women were excluded from the public arena). A citizen had a wife and slaves to take care of many of what we would call the 'practical' aspects of life, even business dealings. The system of slavery left him with some measure of leisure time during which he could become closely involved in the administration of the *polis*, the city-state (Bowra, 1973). So the realm of 'action' for the Athenian citizen was to a large extent the realm of interaction between men, the realm of politics (the affairs of the *polis*). Athens was a democracy, which meant that all citizens participated in and controlled, at least theoretically, the political life of the city (I say 'theoretically' here because often it was the slick and persuasive orators, such as Pericles, who held sway).

For Aristotle the arena of human interaction called forth a particular kind of action — not 'making' action, the form of action in which the artisans engaged, but practical action, *praxis*. In modern (particularly Marxist) thought praxis has come to mean political action in a more radical sense than was meant by the original Greek, so I have reserved the term *praxis* for the sort of critical action which we will examine in relation to the emancipatory interest. I will refer to action associated with the practical interest as 'practical' action.

In discussing the technical interest I asserted that product oriented action, the action associated with the technical interest, arose from a disposition of *techne* or skill. I noted also the association which Habermas makes between the technical disposition and an interest in control. For Aristotle it is the disposition of *phronesis* which gives rise to practical action. The term *phronesis* is often translated as 'practical judgment'. The concept of *phronesis* is a complex one and no single English word is capable of capturing the range of meanings implicit in the original Greek. Knowledge is a component of *phronesis*, but not abstract propositional knowledge, rather knowledge which has its basis in human reason. Knowledge which is formed on the basis of *phronesis* is knowledge which is 'owned' by the actor. By this I mean knowledge which has been made personal in Polanyi's (1962) sense, through reasoning and experience. Judgment is an element of *phronesis*, but not the legalistic judgment of an umpire doggedly making judgments about when infringements of the rules have occurred. What is implied is the judgment of the magistrate who knows when to apply and when to refrain from the application of the full rigour of the law in order that justice may be served (Gadamer, 1979, p. 284). *Phronesis* also involves taste. Taste has to do with what is 'fitting' on a particular occasion:

> [Taste] cannot be separated from the concrete situation on which it operates and cannot be reduced to rules and concepts.... It constitutes a special way of knowing. It belongs in the area of reflective judgment.... Both taste and judgment are evaluations of the object in relation to the whole to see if it fits with everything else, whether, then, it is 'fitting'. (Gadamer, 1979, p. 36)

Phronesis is the basis of the wine-taster's ability. Knowledge, judgment and taste combine to produce a discernment which is more than a skill. I shall generally use the term 'practical judgment' for *phronesis*, but these shades of meaning should be borne in mind because practical judgment is different from strategic judgment which, as we saw previously, is associated with the technical interest.

Techne (skill) produces action which accords with an established rule or traditional way of working. The action follows from a choice between means to achieve a specific, predetermined end. These actions are either the 'purposive-rational' or 'strategic' actions of which

Habermas (1971) speaks. A disposition which utilizes skill is oriented towards correct action; that is, action which either accords with the rule or which is sanctioned by convention. Practical judgment (*phronesis*), on the other hand, according to Aristotle, is 'a true and reasoned disposition toward action with regard to things good and bad for men' (*Nic. Ethics*, 1140b). Practical judgment is a disposition towards 'good' rather than 'correct' action. It possesses an aspect of moral consciousness which the disposition of *techne* lacks. Practical judgment is the disposition which would encourage a person acting in a certain situation to break a rule or convention if he/she judged that to act in accordance with it would not promote 'the good', either generally or of the persons involved in the specific situation. This means that action resulting from practical judgment stands to be evaluated on its own terms rather than by the degree to which it implements a particular 'idea' as is the case with action resulting from *techne*.

Let us ground this difference between action following from skill and from practical judgment in an example. Let us consider the action which a teacher might take as part of introducing an activity-based mathematics programme in his/her class. If that action results from the application of the skills of the teacher to the implementation of the requirements of a syllabus document, the success of the teacher's work will be evaluated by the degree to which the resultant pro-gramme conforms to the specifications of the syllabus. Similar action, occurring as a consequence of the exercising of practical judgment, would be evaluated according to the extent to which it furthers the 'good' of the students. In this case the syllabus document would be regarded as a proposal which could inform the teacher's judgments about what action he/she might take.

This indicates that actions resulting from skill and from practical judgment are qualitatively different. Skill, we saw previously, results in 'making' action. Practical judgment gives rise to interaction (prac-tical action). Practical action (*praxis*) is not random action; it is action 'with regard to human goods' (*Nic. Ethnics*, 1140b). Aristotle sees these two types of human action differing in the following way: 'whereas making (*poietike*) has an end other than itself, action (*praxis*) has not, since well-doing is its own end.' Skill is thus product related, while practical judgment is directed towards the process of taking action. If we apply this to our mathematics class example, the difference is subtle but important. Our teacher whose action is skill-directed will essentially be engaged in constructing a classroom prog-ramme which will produce the learning outcomes required by the syllabus documents. The teacher whose work is informed by practical judgment will be concerned that the interactions of the classroom environment provide appropriate opportunities for learning. The learning moment 'is its own end'.

This does not mean that there is no *eidos* which guides practical action. It was noted above that Aristotle regarded the disposition of practical judgment to be 'a true and reasoned disposition toward action with regard to things good and bad for men.' Thus the *eidos* which guides practical judgment is that of 'the good'. The Greeks were very concerned about 'the good' or moral virtue. 'The good life' for them was not the ideal of sun and surf which is conjured up by that phrase in modern (Australian) society. Rather, it was a concept which combined aesthetic, moral and intellectual meanings associated with that which was beautiful, something 'worthy of warm admiration' (Kitto, 1951). While there will be some consensus among members of any group about the meaning of 'the good', the *eidos* is, nevertheless, also personal, subjective and never fully formed, always in a state of being formed. Gadamer (1979, p. 283) discusses the relationship of this *eidos* to practical action:

> The image that man has of what ought to be i.e. his ideas of right and wrong [etc.] ... are certainly ... guiding ideas towards which he looks: but there is still a basic difference from the guiding idea represented by the plan the craftsman has of an object he is going to make. What is right, for example, cannot be fully determined independently of the situation that requires a right action from me, whereas, the eidos of what a craftsman desires to make is fully determined by the use for which it is intended.

Since what is right cannot be fully determined independently of the situation, practical action is characterized by choice and deliberation. As was noted previously, choice can be involved in 'making', but since it is product, rather than process, directed, the means will be largely determined by the ends; that is, while choice is possible among means, it is restricted. Practical action, however, being centred upon the process of making right decisions which will further 'the good', allows for greater deliberation and hence greater choice of actions since, according to Aristotle, 'we deliberate not about ends but about means' (*Nic. Ethics*, 1112b). For Aristotle the goals of morality were not in question. One did not deliberate, for instance, about whether just action was desirable, only about how to act justly. Deliberation is, thus, an essential element of practical action.

In summary, practical action in the Aristotelian sense is generated by practical judgment, a true disposition towards action based upon the interaction of a personal but shared *eidos* of the 'good' and a given situation. Thus the practical interest is characterized by a general *eidos* of 'the good', a disposition of practical judgment which gives rise to a kind of action which seeks some improvement in a subject or situation. I have represented these relationships among the guiding *eidos*, the disposition and the action in Figure 2, in a similar way as I did for the technical interest. However, this representation does not do justice to the reciprocal relationships of all these components of practical action and so provides only a superficial point of comparison.

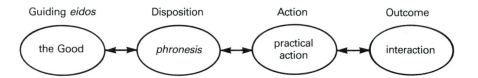

Figure 2. *The Practical Relationship of Ideas and Actions*

We have seen previously that the technical interest had an outcome which was independent of the one taking the action and hence of the actions themselves (the outcome of the technical interest is a product of some kind which exists apart from the producer to the extent that it may have been produced by anyone with the same skills). The practical interest, on the other hand, focuses much more closely upon the act and the actor, rather than upon the outcome of the action. This is a significant difference which needs exploring.

If we go back to the Greeks and ask ourselves what the objective of Greek democracy was, the answer is the welfare of the *polis*, the *polis* being the citizens who comprised the political community. So the desirable outcome of any political decision was a state of being, not a particular result of some kind. This is a rather idealized picture of ancient Greece, but for the moment it is the principle which is instructive for us. The notion of deliberation producing a state of being rather than some final result is illustrated by the tradition that deliberations were never closed. Decisions were never irrevocable in principle. This in practice led to some bizarre occurrences such as military decisions being made today and reversed tomorrow. But there was a real sense in which the decision itself was not of the utmost importance. What was important was that the decision represented the outcome of the deliberations of the citizens.

So the essence of the Greek notion of *praxis* (practical action) was that action should be taken on the basis of a thorough understanding of the situation. Furthermore, it was considered that understanding was achieved only by deliberation and debate through which the meaning of a situation or event became clear. It must be noted, however, with respect to action in the political sphere, that is, the sphere of human interaction, that action is always a risk. The outcome or consequences of action can never be completely known before-hand. There is always an element of risk regarding the unintended outcomes of action. This becomes particularly pertinent to education, as we shall see later.

The practical interest, therefore, generates action *between subjects*, not action *upon objects*. The important thing is to exercise judgment through deliberation (often called 'reflection' in current literature). Deliberation incorporates processes of interpretation and making meaning of a situation so that appropriate action can be decided upon and taken. Appropriate action is that which is deemed to further the 'good' of the participants in the action.

This, then, is why this chapter is entitled 'Curriculum as Prac-tice'. A practical interest at work in curriculum would place the emphasis upon action or practice, rather than upon some product. Furthermore, a practical interest initiates the sort of action which is taken as a consequence of deliberation and a striving to understand or make meaning of the situation on the part of the practitioner rather than action taken as a consequence of a directive or in keeping with some pre-specified objective.

Understanding as Meaning-Making

So far in this chapter I have been talking in a fairly glib way about understanding. We need now to examine this concept more closely to uncover its importance. Let me address the question of the way in which understanding is crucial to the notion of practical action. Why is it not sufficient to require of action in the realm of human affairs that persons act, not out of understanding, but as a consequence of following certain rules or principles? In other words, why is it not sufficient to regard the realm of human interaction as an objective world in which it is possible to identify certain principles which represent the way in which people 'naturally' interact with each other and then to set these up as principles which subsequent communities can act upon in order to reproduce a reasonably efficient form of human society? Although such a set of circumstances would entail a considerable degree of understanding on the part of the originators of the rules of procedure, it would require little understanding on the part of subsequent communities and, hence, being more time efficient and predictable, would be an effective way to conduct human interaction. (Of course, that is how many of our actions in the realm of human affairs are conducted. Consider the rules of etiquette, for example.)

There is a very real sense in which this is the programme of the empirical-analytic human sciences: to 'discover' the 'rules' by which human interaction proceeds and to express these rules or principles in a set of generalizations which can then be used to guide or modify behaviour. Thus, although much understanding is required of those who formulate the 'rules', no fundamental understanding is required to act in accordance with them. What is needed is the skill to see when a particular type of action is appropriate.

The Athenians would have had some problems, I think, accepting this view of the conduct of human affairs. Let us leave alone for a moment whether it is possible to formulate such principles of behaviour or generalizations. The first objection would have been that as a citizen (and thus a human being or a 'man' since those who were not citizens were not regarded as having the status of 'person' in the fullest sense), one had the right, nay, the obligation, to take part in the deliberative and decision-making functions of the *polis*. Merely following rules concocted by another was to be less than human.[1] Not only was there an issue of humanity; there was also one of equality. If all 'men' are equal, then all 'men', not simply a select few, had the right and the responsibility to be involved in decision-making concerning actions to be taken. Of course, we can dismiss these understandings of persons as acting, deliberating beings as the prejudices of a primitive society. However, whether we accept or reject the ancient Athenian position, it presents for us an alternative to the mechanistic view of persons so prevalent in both our society and in many academic analyses of that society. But let us leave aside for a moment the objection that to be a person means to be an active decision-maker, not simply a rule-follower. Let us suppose that in the cause of efficiency or harmony or some other ideal it would be a good idea for persons to yield some of their humanity and their equality for the sake of a commonly perceived goal. They, thus, agree to act in regulated ways for the sake of social goals such as efficiency and harmony.[2] The problem of the application of the rules remains. Even if regularities of action could be identified, human action (along with many other sorts of occurrences in the physical world) is never so predictable that principles can be applied without regard for the uniqueness of any individual event or interaction. The need for probability theory has its origin in this aspect of the physical and human world. Thus, the exercising of judgment based upon an understanding of when it is appropriate to apply the principle of action and when not is still necessary. Gadamer in *Truth and Method* (1979, p. 284) offers the example of the application of law:

> If we think about it, we shall see that the application of the law involves a curious legal ambiguity. The situation of the craftsman is quite different. With the design of the object and the rules of its execution, the craftsman proceeds to carry it out. He may be forced to adapt himself to particular circumstances ... but this does not mean that his knowledge of what he wants is made more perfect. Rather, he simply omits certain things in the execution.... In comparison, the situation of the person who is 'applying' law is quite different. In a specific instance he will have to refrain from applying the full rigour of the law. But if he does, it is not because he has no alternative, but because to do otherwise would not be right. In holding back on the law, he is not diminishing it, but, on the contrary, finding the better law.... Aristotle shows that everything that is set down in law is in a necessary tension with definite action, in that it is general and hence cannot contain within itself practical reality in its full concrete form.

This illustration also rather neatly shows the importance of the link between understanding and meaning-making. Understanding in this case involves making a decision about the meaning of the law and the meaning of the situation under review in relation to the law. Making meaning is both a matter of judgment and is a prerequisite to the exercising of judgment in taking action. But the question remains: How do we establish meaning? The act of establishing meaning is an act of interpretation, and we can gain some instruction in this matter from the practice of interpretation of literary texts.

Gadamer (1979 pp. 236ff) asserts that in trying to understand anything we come to it with certain predispositions and fore-meanings (pre-judgments or prejudices). The process of understanding or interpreting a text is the process of allowing our own prejudices (pre-judgments) to interact with the meaning that the author of the text intended so that the text becomes 'meaningful'.

A person who is trying to understand a text is always per-
forming an act of projecting. He projects before himself a
meaning for the text as a whole as soon as some initial meaning emerges in the text. Again, the latter emerges only because
he is reading the text with particular expectations in regard to
a certain meaning. The working out of the fore-project, which
is constantly revised in terms of what emerges as he penetrates
into the meaning, is understanding what is there.

We have here some interesting relationships. Action in the realm
of human interaction (practical action) is dependent upon judgment,
and the exercising of judgment is dependent upon the interpretation of
the meaning of an event, which, in turn, is dependent upon the
meeting and interaction of the fore-meanings or prejudices of the
participants in the interaction. In the interpretation of a text the
participants are the reader and the written words of the author. In the
interpretation of an event the participants are all those involved in the
event. Thus, practical action presupposes deliberation and negotiation.
Furthermore, this view of interaction incorporates certain implications
concerning the rights and the equality of the participants. In the case
of textual interpretation this concept cuts across the 'tyranny of the
text'; for it presupposes an active meaning-making reader who has as
much right to determine the meaning of the text (though not in
arbitrary or nonsensical ways) as does the author. In the realm of
human interaction it presupposes active meaning-making and, ideally,
equality of participants in an event. In a realm where interaction
occurs between participants who have unequal capacities for understanding or meaning-making, the right of the participants to be
regarded as subjects, not objects in the interaction is acknowledged.
Thus the right of each subject to determine meaning to the extent of
his/her capacity is an important principle to be safeguarded.

Curriculum as Practice

It is time to turn to the implications of what has been discussed for the
curriculum. To speak of the curriculum as belonging in the realm of
the practical is, at one level, to assert no more than that it belongs in
the realm of human interaction, and that the curriculum is concerned
with the interaction between teacher and learners. As soon as this
elementary aspect is recognized, however, some political implications become evident. If we accept that the curriculum is a practical
matter this entails that all participants in the curriculum event are to

be regarded as subjects, not objects. This, in turn, raises issues concerning the participants' rights and status within the event, which also has implications for decision-making regarding the purposes, the content and the conduct of the curriculum.

Let us first consider what is involved if we take a somewhat narrow view of the curriculum, regarding it as a set of documents for implementation. Let us consider, however, the process of curriculum implementation as a practical activity, that is, an activity informed by a practical cognitive interest. The first task which confronts the practitioner in such a situation is that of interpreting the 'curriculum' as text. As was intimated previously, an interpretative view of textual analysis would deny the authority of the document to impose its own meaning. Such a view implies that the practitioner has not only the right, but also the obligation, to make his/her own meaning of the text. In fact, since it is the practitioner who knows the situation in which the provisions of the text are to be applied, it places an obligation upon him/her to do so. This is similar to the obligation which is placed upon the magistrate with respect to the application of the law.

If practitioners take seriously their obligations to regard the interpretation of the curriculum texts as a practical action, that is, as one which engages their judgment, they will also take seriously the status of the students as learning subjects, not objects in the curriculum event. This will mean that learning, not teaching, will be the central concern of the teacher. Moreover, learning will involve, not the production of certain artefacts (whether it is the child or his/her products which are regarded as the artefacts of the education system), but the making of meaning. It would follow from this that such teachers will not only be concerned that they understand the purposes of the prescribed content, but they will reject as legitimate educational content that which does not have at its heart the making of meaning for the learner. In other words, it is not sufficient that the teacher is able to interpret the curriculum texts to come to an understanding of what the document prescribes. For instance, it is not sufficient that a teacher understands that what is intended is for students to undertake learning experiences which will enable them to complete sets of mathematical computations. A teacher whose work is informed by a practical interest will reject mathematics curriculum proposals which encourage the achievement of correct answers as a consequence of the application of appropriate algorithms but fail to make provision for the student actively to engage in making meaning of mathematical problems and their possible solutions.

A further illustration of the difference between a technical and practical interest in curriculum is to be seen in approaches to reading comprehension. When the practice of 'reading comprehension' is informed by a technical interest, the exercise becomes one of decoding a piece of writing to arrive at predetermined answers. When the same practice is informed by a practical interest, the task will be regarded as an interaction between the reader and the author for the generation of meaning. It will no longer be an exercise of ascertaining the author's meaning, but will become an act of personal meaning-making on the part of the reader and one in which the interpretation of that reader is taken seriously.

Such an approach to the curriculum also has implications for how evaluation and assessment are viewed. Since the meaning of the curriculum is a matter of deliberation on the part of the practitioner out of which certain judgments and actions flow, and since the importance of the event is as much in the action or interaction as in the result, then it follows that it no longer makes sense to speak of evaluating the effectiveness of the curriculum in terms of pre-specified objectives. Such objectives, no matter how rationally based upon the understandings and interpretations of the curriculum designers, do not have the authority to determine the practice of the subjects in the interaction. They become what Stenhouse (1975) calls 'hypotheses' to be tested in classroom practice. The participants, both teachers and students, will be involved in the evaluation of curriculum experiences undertaken as a practical activity, for the meanings and interpretations of *all* participants have a claim to being considered in human interaction.

If education is regarded as a practical activity (that is, an activity which takes place through human interaction), we need to ask whether it makes sense at all to regard document-making as 'curriculum design'. Is it sufficient to ascribe to practitioners the role of interpretation, but exclude them from curriculum formulation? What would be the effect if we regarded the whole of the curriculum act as a practical act, that is, as an act of interpretation and meaning-making? What would such a process involve?

The late Lawrence Stenhouse advocated just this approach to the curriculum. In *An Introduction to Curriculum Research and Development* (1975) the principles of a curriculum informed by a practical interest are enunciated. I quote Stenhouse at some length here because he articulates these principles very clearly.

> I have argued that educational ideas expressed in books are not easily taken into possession by teachers, whereas the expression of ideas as curricular specifications exposes them to testing

by teachers and hence establishes an equality of discourse between the proposer and those who assess his proposal. The idea is of an educational science in which each classroom is a laboratory, each teacher a member of the scientific community. There is, of course, no implication as to the origin of the proposal or the hypothesis being tested. The originator may be a classroom teacher, a policy-maker or an educational research worker. The crucial point is that the proposal is not to be regarded as an unqualified recommendation but rather as a provisional specification, claiming no more than to be worth putting to the test of practice. Such proposals claim to be intelligent rather than correct....

Second ... I have identified a curriculum as a particular form of specification about the practice of teaching and not as a package of materials or a syllabus of ground to be covered. It is a way of translating an educational idea into a hypothesis testable in practice. It invites critical testing rather than acceptance.

Finally ... I have reached towards a research design based upon these ideas, implying that a curriculum is a means of studying the problems and effects of implementing any defined line of teaching.... I have argued, however, that the uniqueness of each classroom setting implies that any proposal — even at school level — needs to be tested and verified and adapted by each teacher in his own classroom. The ideal is that the curricular specification should feed a teacher's personal research and development programme through which he is progressively increasing his understanding of his own work, and hence bettering his own teaching. (pp. 142–3)

These curricular principles were enshrined in a national curriculum project focused upon the teaching of race relations. We will examine this project in the following chapter, but let us consider it briefly here as an illustration of the practical interest informing a curriculum project.

The 'givens' for teachers who participated in the project were a set of resource data (pictures, newspaper clippings, stories, etc.) and a choice of teaching strategies. Strategy A required that the teacher adopt the neutral chairing role which had been a feature of the Humanities Curriculum Project (1970). For Strategy B the teacher adopted a committed consensual stance towards the elimination of racial conflict. Strategy C sought to promote understanding of race relations problems through drama. The practical interest inherent in the conceptualization of this project is evident in a comment made elsewhere by Stenhouse (1975, p. 130):

> Experience in the field of curriculum suggests to us that the contextual variables in the school and its environment are so important that there can be no basis for general recommendations. Each school will have to assess its own problems and evolve its own policy. A research on problems and effects of teaching about race relations should concentrate on collecting the data which schools will need to support them in the exercising of their judgment.

Interestingly, the same research stance was adopted for the dissemination of the curriculum approach. In a document describing the dissemination process Rudduck and Stenhouse (1979, p. 4) provide the following rationale for the method of dissemination:

> The [dissemination] project ... is based ... [on the] assumption that its work cannot be applied without [teachers] adopting the research and development attitudes to their teaching which teachers have achieved within the framework of the experimental phase of the project.

This being so, it was agreed that the dissemination of the race project should be based on the experiences of teachers and these were best communicated by the teachers themselves rather than, for instance, curriculum consultants or advisory teachers.

The practical knowledge-constitutive interest is most clearly perceivable in this curriculum project through the high value placed upon personal judgment. This meant that whatever knowledge or insights were generated by the project as a whole or by the systematic reflections of the participating teacher, these had no deterministic implications for the teacher's future actions in his/her own classroom. At all times the interpretation of both actions and findings was to be subject to the practitioner's judgment. This practical interest which centralizes the importance of *phronesis* (practical judgment) in the generation and application of knowledge permeates Stenhouse's work. The following passage expresses this respect for judgment even in the face of 'hard' research evidence:

> In reporting research I am hoping to persuade you to review your own experience critically and then test the research

against your critical assessment of that experience. I am not seeking to claim that the research should override your judgment: it should supplement it and enrich it.... Looking at any research findings in these terms there are two questions that you will have to ask yourselves: first, is it generally true? and second, is it true in my case? (Rudduck and Stenhouse, 1979, pp. 81,82)

This project did attempt to measure changes in attitudes on the part of the students, that is, to measure what the project had produced, but the results were inconclusive. Stenhouse's insistence upon personal judgment is due to more than the inconclusive nature of the findings. Even if the results were statistically unambiguous, they could still present no more than a series of hypotheses that would have to be tested in individual classrooms.

Persons and the Practical Interest

One of the principles inherent in the practical interest is that persons, including children, are fundamentally rational. Nevertheless, it is acknowledged that principles of freedom, if adhered to, may result in unintended outcomes such as the hardening of racist attitudes. Stenhouse acknowledges the riskiness of this joint commitment to freedom and rationality:

Some pupils are becoming more racist during the teaching. If this were not the situation, then the world would never have conceived of brain-washing: education would be enough to convert anyone to any view, at least any which could be rationally justified. (Rudduck and Stenhouse, 1979, p. 83)

Evidence of this commitment to rationality is to be found in the firm belief in the prudent, discerning capacity of personal judgment exercised through systematic processes of reflection. These processes of reflection are initiated as a teacher systematically examines and refines or modifies his/her practice.

This commitment to rationality which is discernible in Stenhouse's work and which is consistent with the practical interest is also discernible in Dewey's work. In *How We Think* (1933) Dewey wrote: '... A man of sound judgment in any set of affairs is an *educated* man as respects those affairs whatever his schooling or academic standing.'

Curriculum Issues

One of the problems with taking a different perspective on the curriculum is that traditional ways of thinking about curriculum processes do not always apply. But let me try to get some comparative perspective into the discussion by considering what a practical view of curriculum means when considered from the perspective of the traditional categories of curriculum discourse which were used to discuss the technical interest.

The Nature of the Eidos

In discussing curriculum as product I noted that the technical requirement of a pre-specified *eidos* which depends upon the *techne* of the practitioner for its realization is parallel to the traditional view of curriculum which requires specific, pre-planned objectives for implementation through the skill of the practitioner. The practical cognitive interest presupposes a much more general *eidos*: the notion of the 'good' and it is dependent upon the judgment of the practitioner as to how that *eidos* is interpreted and translated into action.

This *eidos* is discernible in the Race Relations Project. There the project was guided by general notions of the 'good' rather than a predetermined set of attitudes from a package of knowledge to be passed on. This 'good' encompassed desirable attitudes of racial tolerance and interracial harmony as well as a commitment to freedom and rationality. The *eidos* was not, however, a simple set of desirable attitudes; it was acknowledged as complex and sometimes contradictory. One of the teachers who was involved in the project explains the tentative nature of the guiding *eidos*: 'It is an assumption that it does do good, even though it's implicitly valuing any opinion ... but the outcome I think in theory, is racial tolerance' (Rudduck, 1975, p. 78). This quotation also illustrates the desired consequence of the action of teaching: an improvement in the state of the client. The relationship between *eidos* and consequence is, however, also problematic. Practical judgment rather than skill is the valued disposition. Even the strategies serve only to suggest approaches to be taken; they do not function as a 'method': 'I don't think we'd go so far as to say that one strategy was the right way to deal with the topic of race relations, because our research doesn't indicate that any one is more successful than another' (Rudduck, 1976, p. 83). The absence of method emphasizes the value placed upon judgment. It is important to note, however, that judgment does not have a one-dimensional link with action. Rather, judgment and action are reciprocally related through a process of reflection. This means that the practitioner is engaged in deliberative, choosing action guided by personal judgment. Such action becomes a form of *praxis*.

Responsibility and Division of Labour

We noted with respect to the technical interest that there was a separation implied between designer and 'artisan'. In the curriculum process this translates into a division between developers and implementers. No such division is envisaged by the practical interest. Stenhouse (1975, pp. 142–3) says: '[An educational proposal is] not to be regarded as an unqualified recommendation, but rather as a provisional specification claiming no more than to be worth putting into practice.' And again: 'It is not enough that teachers' work should be studied: they need to study it themselves.'

This does not mean that, as well as having to bear the burden of all the work associated with catering for the learning of their students, I am advocating that teachers should also have sole responsibility for initiating educational reform and curriculum change. Such a view woruld entail an unacceptable increase in the intensification of teachers' work. Rather, the industrial implications of the practical interest are that teacher participation in curriculum decision-making is not simply desirable, but is unavoidable. Thus, teachers have a legitimate claim for involvement in all aspects of curriculum development to whatever degree is possible, given the other demands upon their time.

The Importance of Judgment

We have considered the centrality of judgment to the practical curriculum process in some detail above so need here only to highlight some of the points made previously. When a practical cognitive interest informs curriculum practices, although those practices are facilitated by the skills of the teacher, they are much more dependent upon the exercising of judgment. Judgment is not a skill but it can be developed through processes of reflection.

Although the work of Stenhouse has been used here to provide practical examples of the centrality of reflection and deliberation to practical curriculum processes, there has been a general emphasis in recent curriculum literature upon the importance of deliberation and reflection in curriculum development. This has been particularly evident following Schwab's (1969) paper arguing for a return to 'the practical' as a basis for curriculum decision-making.[3]

Curriculum Content

A practical cognitive interest will mean that curriculum content will be determined by considerations of the 'good' rather than what is to be taught being selected in order to achieve a set of pre-specified ends. Because the emphasis in any selection of content will be upon meaning-making and interpretation, it is likely that content will tend to be holistically oriented and integrated, rather than fragmented and subject-specific. At the very least, the division of content into rigid subject specializations would come under scrutiny as to whether such divisions are the best way of making meaning of the knowledge store of the society. Curriculum content would, thus, encourage interpretation and the exercising of judgment by the learner as well as the teacher, rather than encouraging rote learning the demonstration of pre-specified skills.

Stenhouse (1975, p. 86) claims that '... it is quite possible to evolve principles for the selection of content in the curriculum in terms of criteria which are not dependent on the existence of a specification of objectives, and which are sufficiently specific to give real guidance....' He then proceeds to explicate these principles by examining what teachers might do in the act of teaching. Thus it is that he proposes 'a process model' of teaching and learning which 'rests on teacher judgment rather than on teacher direction' (p. 96).

The 'practical' curriculum is not, however, a contentless curriculum: it is a curriculum in which the content is never taken for granted. Content must always be justified in terms of moral criteria relating to 'the good', not simply justified cognitively.

The Meaning of Evaluation

Just as development and implementation of curriculum cannot be completely separated where a practical cognitive interest exists, so also evaluation becomes very much an integral part of the whole educative process, not a separate part. Stenhouse (1975, p. 121) says: 'I want to argue against the separation of developer and evaluator and in favour of integrated curriculum research.' When the technical interest predominates, evaluation means assessing the effectiveness of the curriculum in terms of the extent to which the product 'matched' the guiding *eidos*. Given a practical interest, therefore, evaluation will mean making judgments about the extent to which the process and the practices undertaken through the learning experience furthered the 'good' of all participants. These are not judgments which can be made entirely by those outside the teaching situation for they require the sort of personal knowledge to which only the participants in the learning situation can have access. The insights of others are valuable for reflection, but ultimately the practical interest requires that the participants be the judges of their own actions.

Drawing Together

The technical and practical interests which inform curriculum practices are sometimes interpreted as simply 'process' and 'product' approaches. The distinctions are, however, a little more subtle than that because 'process' approaches to curriculum have so often become technologized. For example, science education in many cases has moved away from an emphasis upon factual recall to an emphasis upon 'processes of discovery' and 'problem-solving'. However, what has tended to happen is that scientific processes have been reduced to a set of skills that students need in order to act scientifically, for example, to light a bunsen burner. When the student is able to demonstrate certain skills, he/she is deemed to have accomplished the process. The actions have become the ends; the processes have become the product. Whether or not the student is able to apply the skills to make sense of the world around him/her is somehow overlooked. In the previous chapter we saw how 'process writing', which is supposed to provide students with an understanding of what it means to be a writer, has tended to be reduced to a rigid set of steps to follow. The process is coopted to serve production objectives. We must be careful that, when we talk about 'process' approaches to the curriculum, we place deliberation, judgment and meaning-making as central. Otherwise we will have slipped into a technical mode. On the other hand, a recognition of the importance of deliberation and judgment-making can be the basis upon which the learning experience becomes more meaningful for both student and teacher.

Notes

1   For an interesting discussion of the place of law in Athenian society see Bowra (1973), chapter 4. Chapter 5 also provides an instructive account of what the Greeks meant by 'the good man' and 'the good life'.
2   This is essentially what Hobbes was proposing through the notion of the social contract. Nowell-Smith (1954, p. 17) notes that 'Hobbes was much impressed by the method of geometry and he thought that moral rules were Rules found out by Reason for avoiding social calamity.'
3   See, for instance, a number of papers in the *Journal of Curriculum Studies* in the mid-1980s, for example, Harris (1986), Orpwood (1985), Roby (1985).

Chapter 5

Practical Curriculum Development

In this chapter I shall examine in some detail two British curriculum projects in which a practical interest is discernible. I shall then outline how a practical interest exhibits itself in the way in which some other teachers talk about and report their work. One of the British projects to be examined is the project which disseminated the Race Relations Curriculum proposals discussed in the previous chapter. I have chosen to concentrate upon the dissemination project for two reasons. The first is that the report of the Race Relations Curriculum Development Project is publicly available elsewhere (Stenhouse *et al.*, 1982). A more important consideration is that the dissemination project was carried out by the teachers who had been involved in the development project. The dissemination reports contain a record of the knowledge which these teachers sought to pass on to other teachers. It is thus in the ways in which the project is reported in its dissemination phase that the practical interest is most convincingly discernible. The other major curriculum project to be discussed in this chapter is the Ford Teaching Project, directed by John Elliott through the Cambridge Institute of Education.

Dissemination of the Race Relations Project

This discussion of the project is based upon an archive of five case records compiled by Jean Rudduck (1975–78), the evaluator of the project, and a final report jointly authored by Rudduck and Stenhouse (1979). (When quotations are given from these sources, the abbreviation C.R. will refer to one of the Case Records and F.R. to the Final Report.)

The original Race Relations Curriculum Development Project

was conducted in forty schools, involving over 100 teachers. (I shall refer to the teachers who took part in the original project as the 'project teachers' and the teachers to whom they were disseminating the project as the 'interested teachers'.) The teachers taking part in the project adopted one of the three strategies outlined in the previous chapter: a neutral chairing role, a committed stance towards the elimination of racial tension, or the strategy of teaching about race relations through drama. It was noted in the previous chapter that Stenhouse emphasized the importance of practitioner judgment in the development of curriculum:

> Experience in the field of curriculum suggests to us that the contextual variables in the school and its environment are so important that there can be no basis for general recommendations.... A research on problems and effects about teaching about race relations should concentrate on collecting the data which schools will need to support them in the exercising of their judgment. (1975, p. 130)

The same research stance was adopted in relation to dissemination. It was agreed that the dissemination of the Race Relations Project should be based upon the experiences of teachers and that these were best communicated by the teachers themselves. In trying to tease out evidence of the practical interest which is implied by this research stance towards curriculum development, we shall examine the knowledge and the action which were generated by the project and discussed by the project teachers.

The Race Relations Project had generated both *content* and *conduct* knowledge for the participants; that is, knowledge of *what* such a curriculum should comprise and knowledge about *how* to go about investigating the curriculum proposals in action. Conduct knowledge, that is, knowledge which related to the actions in which they engaged, was regarded as most important by the 'project teachers'. The 'interested teachers' who attended the various dissemination conferences were more concerned with 'the results' of the teaching. This implies a different cognitive interest between the two groups. The concerns of the 'project teachers' indicate a practical interest in action, whilst the concerns of the 'interested teachers' are indicative of a technical interest in products.

The difference in emphasis referred to above is illustrated in the following exchange. The 'interested teachers' kept pushing for something almost tangible to take away with them, but the 'project teachers' wanted to convey an attitude rather than a set of ideas:

Interested Teacher: ... but you say that you have something to disseminate. You feel that there are some experiences that you should be passing on. Now presumably some of it is more than simply saying 'You have to sort this out for yourself first'.

Jimmy (Project Teacher): Yes ... but I fear what happens so often with exercises like this is 'There it is; there is what happened', and you go away with that bit, that bit, that bit. (C.R. 3, p. 107)

There is a tension here and in other parts of the transcript from which this exchange is extracted. Jimmy is reluctant simply to state what he did in his classroom. He is unable to divorce discussion of the strategies employed from a consideration of the interactive process which preceded his adoption of the particular strategy. The teachers to whom he is speaking, however, are more interested in what he did and what the results were, rather than why or in what circumstances he came to do what he did. This difference between the disseminators and the receivers is highlighted by Rudduck who identifies the following tendencies in the 'interested teachers':

- a tendency to value the teacher-disseminators as raconteurs of their classroom experience rather than as critics of their classroom experience.
- a tendency to rely on teaching materials as the key to classroom change
- a tendency ... to want more assurance about the good effects of teaching about race relations in their own classrooms than research that recognizes the individuality of classrooms. (F.R., p. 130)

The 'interested teachers' exhibited a technical cognitive interest through their concern with product and their hesitancy about relying upon judgment. This contrasts with the emphasis which the 'project teachers' placed upon judgment. They stressed that the context of the action must be taken into account rather than judgments being made on the results of decontextualized action. The sort of knowledge which was important to the 'project teachers' was knowledge which is informed by a practical interest. This interest is even more evident in the level of control which the 'project teachers' exhibited with respect to the knowledge which the project generated.

The 'project teachers' exhibited a level of understanding, grounded in reflection, which makes possible shared meanings. These meanings are not imposed upon the teachers, but are developed through the exercising of personal judgment in relation to their own practice. It is this high value placed upon personal judgment which most clearly indicates a practical cognitive interest. This meant that whatever knowledge or insights were generated by the project as a whole, or by the systematic reflections of a participating teacher, these had no authority to determine future actions of teachers adopting the Race Relations curriculum proposal. At all times the interpretation of action and findings was to be subject to the practitioner's judgment.

Another aspect of the practical cognitive interest which was discussed in the previous chapter was the nature of the *eidos* which guides action. In the case of the practical interest this is a general notion of 'the Good', which means that action is understood to provide for some improvement in the human condition. The nature and extent of that improvement are again a matter of practitioner judgment.

In the Race Relations Project 'the good' encompassed desirable attitudes of racial tolerance and interracial harmony as well as a commitment to freedom and rationality. This *eidos* is not a simple set of desirable attitudes to be imparted to students. It is acknowledged as complex and sometimes contradictory. This complexity is expressed by one of the 'project teachers' when discussing the neutral chairman strategy:

> Dave: . . . [there] is an assumption, yes, that it does do good,
> even though it's implicitly valuing any opinion
> . . . but the outcome I think in theory, is racial
> tolerance. (C.R.4, p. 78)

The relationship here between the guiding *eidos*, 'doing some good' and the consequence of racial tolerance is also problematic. Judgment rather than skill is the valued disposition. Even the teaching strategies serve only to suggest approaches to be taken. They do not function as a 'method': 'I don't think we'd go so far as to say that one strategy was the right way to deal with the topic of race relations, because our research doesn't indicate that any one is more successful than another' (C.R.2, p. 83).

Although judgment is centrally important in this project, it does not have a one-dimensional link with action. Rather judgment and action are reciprocally linked through reflection (C.R.2, p. 77). This means that the teacher is engaged in deliberative, choosing action guided by personal judgment. The process of reflection was made systematic in this project through the teachers' use of action research through which they monitored and moulded their teaching (C.R.4, p. 16).

I mentioned previously that the practical interest of the 'project teachers' became even more evident when the technical interest of the 'interested teachers' is recognized. Furthermore, the interpretation that this project was informed by a practical and not an emancipatory interest is supported by the lack of a critical focus for the project. The actions of the teachers were directed towards psychological, not social change. It was student attitudes, not the material contextual conditions which were the focus for improvement. The lack of a socially critical perspective was not a matter of oversight, it was quite deliberate on the part of the project director. Stenhouse saw the project as a conscious effort to engage in a pedagogical experiment, not in theoretical debate (F.R., p. 105). At least one teacher was alienated from the project by this lack of ideological critique (F.R., p. 85). However, this absence of a critical perspective was held to be a strength by one commentator on the project:

> The teachers captured on audio or video-tape their attempts to implement, that is to test, the hypotheses in practice. And their practice infused with a hypothetical praxis displays issues to the professional audience without the refraction of social theory. (May, 1981, p. 10)

There is no evidence in any of the documents of any teacher or class taking strategic action directed towards change in the structure or organization of the school. While freedom is a value stance implicit in each of the proposed strategies, especially the neutral chairman role, the project itself was not informed by an emancipatory cognitive interest.

The practical interest of this curriculum project is, therefore, identifiable both through the presence of aspects such as judgment and deliberation and by the absence of other features which would identify predominantly either a technical or an emancipatory interest.

The Ford Teaching Project

This project was directed by John Elliott, a former member of the Stenhouse Humanities Curriculum Project. It is not surprising that this project should also be one in which a practical cognitive interest is in evidence. May describes the intentions of the Ford Teaching Project in the following way:

> [It] aimed to help teachers already attempting to implement
> inquiry-discovery methods, but aware of a gap between
> attempt and achievement, to narrow this gap by fostering an
> action research orientation towards classroom problems....
> Thus the team sought to assist teachers adopting such a stance
> by helping them to master techniques for studying process in
> their classrooms. The phrase used was 'self-monitoring
> teachers'. (May, 1981, p. 12)

It was intended that teachers would ultimately use the process of
self-monitoring independently in their classrooms. In the project,
however, self-monitoring was conducted in conjunction with an
observer or a 'facilitator' (that is, one who facilitated the reflections of
the teacher). One technique used for self-monitoring was 'triangulation', which Elliott describes as follows:

> ... triangulation procedures ... constituted an attempt to
> engage teachers in a form of practical discourse about the
> meanings implicit in their teaching acts. They involved the
> production and collection of accounts of classroom processes
> from the points of view of the teacher, the student, and an
> observer. The accounts were then compared and contrasted by
> the teacher in discussion with the other parties and in the light
> of observable data captured in audio and audio-visual record-
> ings. (Elliott, 1983, p. 23)

These comments by both May and Elliott suggest the practical interest of the project, for the concern is with teachers' knowledge, and
the site for the production of that knowledge is the classroom, the site
of the teacher's practice.

The teachers who became involved in the project were already
committed to the notion of enquiry/discovery learning, but, as May
noted, were 'aware of the gap between attempt and achievement'. The
knowledge produced through participation was about the teacher's
own practice, not primarily the content of the students' learning. The
knowledge that teachers gained, however, came not only from self-
monitoring their own practice, but also through dialogue with the
project facilitators and other teachers and, more rigorously, by testing
the hypotheses that had been developed through the investigations of
other teachers (Elliott and Hurlin, 1975, pp. 4f).

The knowledge which was generated from the project was
primarily interpretative. Written evidence in the form of lesson transcripts and observer notes as well as visual evidence in the form of

photographs and slides provided the documents to be interpreted by the practitioners. The interpretative knowledge base seems to perpetuate the influence of Stenhouse the historian, and the concern to wed this interpretative framework to a logical analysis (Elliott and Adelman, 1975, pp. 10ff) reflects the influence of Elliott, the philosopher, upon the concerns of the project. The interpretative epistemology is also reflected in the offering of 'hypotheses' as the outcomes of the project rather than 'findings'.

An example of a specific investigative procedure by one of the teachers, David Partington, illustrates the way in which curriculum development in this project was wedded to improvement in the teachers' practices through processes of deliberation, rather than being regarded as a set of learning outcomes. This description is based upon an account entitled *Three Points of View in the Classroom*, written by Elliott and Partington.

The context of this investigation was a discussion by a group of fifth-year secondary students of their findings from an experiment on the effects of different treatments on plant growth. A tape recording was made of the lesson in which the discussion took place. Elliott sat outside the group, making rapid impressionistic notes while the discussion was in progress. Immediately after the lesson Elliott interviewed the teacher and then the students, checking his observations against theirs. These interviews were also recorded and transcribed. A final discussion chaired by the observer between the teacher (who had heard the tape of the observer/student discussion) and the students was later held. This final discussion was also taped. (This is the triangulation procedure referred to above.)

Some time after these events, without referring to any of the post-lesson discussions or observer notes, the observer analyzed the lesson transcript, 'to see whether any worthwhile interpretations can be made retrospectively, relying solely upon memory and transcript' (Elliott and Partington, 1975, p. 2). Finally Elliott studied all the documentation of the lesson in order to identify the main teaching problems. The points identified then became the basis for generating experimental teaching strategies to resolve the classroom problems.

The knowledge which was generated by the participants in this project can be identified as being informed by a practical cognitive interest. The first grounds for this claim are to be found in the importance placed upon the practitioners' knowledge. The project was not about imparting knowledge of how to go about doing enquiry/discovery teaching, it was about creating situations in which practitioners could develop their own practical knowledge. But this self-generated knowledge was not skill knowledge. Rather, it was understanding which arose from processes of action and reflection. Hurlin, one of the teachers in the project, provides an example of this. He portrays participation in the project as a learning experience in which the teachers, not the project directors determined the direction of the project:

> On reflection, I think we tried too much too soon. The recognition of our aim was one thing, but the realization of it was clearly another.... We are fortunate indeed that we are together for another year and we will have time to explore further what we have begun doing in Inquiry/Discovery work. (Hurlin, 1975, p. 27)

This statement implies a practical interest in a number of ways. Notice first that the riskiness of decisions in the realm of practice is in evidence. It was not possible accurately to predict beforehand what was achievable. But improvement was more important than achieving a pre-specified outcome, and improvement was judged to have occurred. Notice, too, that the work was collaborative and deliberative. These aspects are evidence of a practical interest.

The claim that knowledge was self-generated is, however, problematic in the light of the clear role of the observer outlined in the description of Partington's investigations. The classroom observers provided a service role for the teachers by 'capturing' and documenting the actions of the classroom for later reflection. In the deliberative phase of the investigations they then adopted a Socratic function, probing and clarifying the participants' responses to generate hypotheses for further investigation. Although this non-directive role was implicit in the processes of the project (indeed, the observers were fostering with the teachers just the sort of enquiry strategies with respect to their own practice that the teachers were wanting to foster with their students), the power relationships between facilitator and practitioner were not as symmetrical as the above description would suggest. When the transcripts of the discussions are analyzed it is evident that it is the observer, not the teacher, who usually identified the issues for discussion. At other times it is clear from the pattern of talk that it is the facilitator who is directing the discussion and lapsing into an instructional rather than a discussion mode. This is the case, for instance, in an account entitled *Social Studies in the Secondary School*, where in the post-lesson interview the practitioner's responses become short and defensive while the facilitator embarks on extended speeches.

There is some evidence that the teachers were not intimidated by the power of the observer. On the contrary, as teachers learnt to examine the documentary evidence of their practice they often challenged the interpretations of the observers. Tony Hurlin (1975, p. 17), for instance, wrote:

> Some conflict of operation arises here. John Elliott feels that we did use [pseudo-questions], and I feel that we certainly didn't. I have been delighted to have been unable to locate any evidence for this in the transcripts. Basically a pretence on our part would have been incompatible with our general aim of openness with the children.

The practical interest which is evident in the reports of these two projects is characteristic of much British curriculum work. It is work which places a high value upon the way in which teachers can develop their own understandings of their practice. In the light of these understandings they are able to formulate plans for the improvement of their practice and for making the learning of their students more meaningful. But lest this interest in understanding the learning environment through the development of consensual interpretations of meaning be thought to be a fundamental British characteristic, let us consider the work of some other teachers. I shall use some of the written and spoken insights of teachers who were involved in the projects described in chapter 3 above, particularly the Karrivale project, to disclose evidence of a practical interest. As well as these projects I shall make reference to two other school-based curriculum development projects: Martin Valley High School and Mount Barden Primary School. Profiles of these projects are provided below. For the sake of providing a basis for more direct comparisons with previous and later chapters dealing with examples of work informed by technical and emancipatory interests, I shall also organize this discussion in a similar way to the structure of chapter 3. We shall consider, with respect to knowledge, the nature of the knowledge generated, the value ascribed to theory and the theory/practice relationship and, with respect to action, the focus, target and quality of the action in which the teachers engaged.

Other Project Profiles

Martin Valley High School

Despite the fact that Martin Valley had recently been involved in a whole school evaluation, there was a feeling within the school, prior to the school-based curriculum development being embarked upon, that they were functioning at a level of expediency and engaging in *ad hoc* decision-making. They invited a curriculum consultant to work with them. She did so over the next two years.

During the first year three significant issues emerged. One was the size of the school and the effect that this had on both students and staff. The second related to the contrasts between the high school and the smaller primary schools from which students came. This issue related both to school size and to the appropriateness of the year 8 programme. The third issue concerned the structure of knowledge and theories of learning.

At the end of the first year the decision was made to establish sub-schools. The organization of the school into smaller administrative and pedagogical units opened up opportunities for improvement in learning through the possibility of improved relationships with students. Subsequent to this decision the curriculum consultant worked with a group of eight teachers who wanted systematically to examine and change aspects of their practice which the reorganization of the school facilitated. These included experimenting with negotiating the curriculum with students and fostering improvements in interpersonal relationships.

Mount Barden Primary School

At Mount Barden Primary School a group of teachers agreed to investigate the language development of the students in their classrooms. Within this framework teachers made selections of particular areas of focus which interested them and which they believed were important in the language development of their students. They agreed to observe what already existed in their classrooms and to try out an idea which would involve a change in their practice.

Included in the group were the principal, who was concerned with school-wide implications of a focus upon language and its links with teacher development, and a deputy principal who coordinated a Language Arts Committee, formed as a nucleus for school-based in-service within the programme. All participating teachers agreed to document their observations and experiences over a period.

Looking into the Projects

Knowledge Generated

The practical interest gives rise to prudent and meaningful action. Such action does not occur as a consequence of following a set of 'rules for action', however. It has as its base the understanding of the meaning of the situation by the practitioner. Such understanding is not simply an *ad hoc* matter arising out of an instantaneous 'summing up' of the situation. It arises from reflective deliberation upon the situation, upon previous action and upon theoretical explanations which may assist interpretation.

When teachers begin to take a reflective stance towards their work they become aware of the development of their own understanding. Two of the Karrivale teachers expressed this awareness of developing understanding. Frank talked about the change in himself from a concern simply with outcome to a concern for the learning experience:

> Before, I used to have a programme or unit and it worked and I used to say: 'Oh, that's a good programme, I'll use it again', rather than thinking, 'Well why did that one work and that one not? ' I thought it was the programme.... Now that I've started going back and looking at why they work, I've begun to realize ... the type of learning that's going on....

Peter expressed his questioning of 'technical' (or product determined) ways of working in the following way:

> A lot of the time ... you've got your aims and objectives to achieve ... and you want to get through them [but] in this sort of process you forget about your objectives and you concentrate on how you're doing things.... The way you're doing it is something you have to stop and look at very critically and work on. So that was specifically something that I think impressed my understanding.

Recognizing the importance of understanding, however, means that sharing ideas with others becomes problematical. Understanding is something which is acquired, not simply picked up. Nancy reflected upon this dilemma: 'I'm a bit worried that some people still don't understand group work, they still don't understand journals and they still don't understand draft work; but I guess it's going to take time.' This expresses the crucial difference between developing understanding and gaining ideas. While the latter can be picked up and applied instantly, the gaining of understanding is a long process. Viv talked of a 'stumbling towards realization' by those engaged in examining their practice. For her the growth in her understanding represented 'a movement, from my initial adoption of one English teaching fashion ... towards a more informed personal choice.'

Often critics of an investigative and reflective approach to development of practice worry about teachers 're-inventing the wheel'. Ed rejected this as a legitimate concern:

> People, in my view have to learn things for themselves, one by one.... You can't just say, 'Here, this is what I know, read this and you'll know it.' ... You need to go through the same sort of experience, then you learn something that might be similar or might be different ... but it will mean something to you.

This also means that practical knowledge of this sort is not necessarily new knowledge for the world, but it is new for the practitioner.

The teachers engaged in these projects exhibited a range of understandings in a variety of areas. Glenda, a teacher at Martin Valley, reflected upon the understanding of her own practice:

> I find myself asking things like: 'Why do we always just load on them? Why don't we get them to participate? Why do we do what we do in science?'

Pete, another teacher at the same school, reflected upon his growing understanding of his students:

> I'm more tolerant of things that happen, I can understand because I tend to get more knowledge about the kids, and I can understand if they blow their top off.... Once you can reflect on things ... and really get down to exactly what is the problem ... [you can] develop the idea of personal action plans for the kids.

A teacher in the Language Development Project reflected upon her developing understanding of her students' learning capacities:

> After completing this research I now had a much clearer idea of ... which children needed more help to get started, which were averse to writing ... and I also discovered that several were using oral vocabulary far beyond their written capabilities.

Wendy, a teacher in the Karrivale project, reflected upon her developing understanding of the students' learning processes:

> When I asked a couple of them to explain what they meant, I discovered that they were reacting to their prediction not having matched what eventually happened in the story. This was an important insight and a breakthrough in my understanding of the significance of prediction.

Yvonne, a teacher at Mount Barden, sums up most succinctly the scope of the understandings that may be generated for teachers through processes of reflection upon their practice:

> In looking at children and why they write, I have started to gain insights into the way children learn in general, and the conditions necessary for true learning to take place. This means that my classroom organization, my planning and my programming are now no longer completely suitable for the learning needs of children.

Theory

Gaining the sort of practical understanding of their work which is evidenced in the above statements of the teachers is only one aspect of the generation of knowledge through the practical interest. As well as knowledge arising directly through reflection upon practice, the practical interest encourages the development of knowledge through the bringing to consciousness of implicit theory and thus providing a more consciously rational basis for action. The philosopher Gadamer (1977, p. 38) acknowledges the power of reflection as being that of bringing to consciousness that which is implicitly and unquestioningly accepted: 'The real power of hermeneutic consciousness is our ability to see what is questionable.... Reflection on a given pre-understanding brings before me something that otherwise happens behind my back.' Such reflection is indicative of a practical cognitive interest and is strongly evident in the self-reports of the teachers whose work we are considering here. The theory which these teachers value is their own implicit theory which has been made explicit through reflection. The implicit theory may be the traditional wisdom of the profession which has been tacitly accepted and internalized or practical theories about ways of working developed and internalized through years of experience. Wendy, one of the Karrivale teachers, for instance, expressed in her writing a growing realization that many of her habitual ways of working in the classroom actually sprang from 'sound theory':

> When I was a beginning teacher ... I developed ... a repertoire of what I considered to be tricks and gimmicks for keeping my classes in order.... What I didn't realize was that some of my 'tricks' were in fact the basis for strategies which I would later come to recognize as having their roots in sound theory.

Janice, another teacher working in the same project, acknowledged in her writing that many of the understandings she developed through systematic exploration and reflection had been implicit in her earlier work: 'It was only when planning this strategy that I really re-discovered my earlier recorded journal ideas, and realized that I'd been heading in this direction all the time.'

Reflection, such as that described by Wendy and Janice, can give retrospective meaning to past practice or meaning to prospective practice by bringing assumptions and values to consciousness. This prospective value of reflection was intimated in an interview with Mike, one of the teachers in the Investigating Learning Project. 'Right from the start,' he noted, 'whatever it is that you're looking at or doing, you should be explicit about what your values and assumptions are.' This involves retrospective reflection as well as prospective deliberation. Mike noted also the importance of coming to understand the implicit assumptions of past practice:

> The whole thing was a process of making this tacit feeling explicit, but at a lower level, you've got to think: 'well I do this and I do that tacitly, I do it without thinking about it.' [You've] got to take stock and make explicit what is deeply embedded.

One of the ways in which these teachers found that they were able to make that which was 'happening behind their backs' explicit to themselves was through the act of writing. Wendy found that writing about her practice gave her analytical insights into what was occurring in her classes: 'I find myself looking at what [the students] have done in terms of how I would explain this if I had to write it up. What can I really see happening?' Glenda, from Martin Valley High, also attested the value of writing as a means of making the implicit basis of her work explicit to herself: 'Just the writing down, I guess because its slow or something, you're reflecting on what's happened and I'm sure I picked up a lot of good things that were happening that I wouldn't have otherwise done.' Pete, a teacher who worked with the Karrivale project, noted that sharing insights with other teachers through writing about your work 'makes you search inside yourself.' Sam, a teacher in the same project, reflected in the following way about his experience of making the implicit explicit through the act of writing: 'When I'd written [the account] and then reflected on that whole year, the threads which were coming together, the insights, the tacit understandings ... even when I was writing it, they started to come together.'

Theory/Practice

The practical interest has one other implication for the knowledge of teachers working in this mode, in relation to the theory/practice link. It was noted with respect to the technical interest that theory can have a deterministic relationship to practice. The practical interet, however, encourages a much greater degree of control of both theory and practice by practitioners. For the teacher whose work is informed by a practical interest, theoretical statements have the status of proposals for action, not prescriptions. Furthermore, it is the practitioner who makes decisions about the applicability of such proposals to the practical situation. This representation of 'theory' as providing guidance, not direction is evident in a comment made by Wendy in interview:

> I don't really see myself as a formulator of theory, but I do feel confident that I can adapt perhaps existing theory to suit just my own classroom ... to take as much of the theory as I think is relevant to my students or to what I want to do.

Here the emphasis upon 'application' in the sense of hermeneutic application discussed in the previous chapter is evident. There is also a strong sense of the importance of the teacher's judgment, not simply to judge when the application of certain proposals is warranted, but also just what aspects of the proposal are appropriate. A theory/practice relationship such as this provides for greater opportunity for decision-making on the part of the practitioner than does a technical interest which casts the practitioner as the implementer of theory. In the explanation by Frank, another of the Karrivale teachers, of the way in which theoretical proposals for classroom action need to be subject to reflection and evaluation by the practitioner, this aspect of the implication of the practical interest is also evident:

> The rationale for negotiation is a case in point; it is persuasive because it is clearly sound in what it says. It is true that if students can develop a sense of ownership of their work ... significant learning will occur.... The crucial question ... is 'What are the problems in implementing this enticing and desirable goal of having students assume responsibility for much of their learning?'

If these are the ways in which teachers whose work is informed by a practical interest understand both their practice and the theoretical explanations of and proposals relating to that practice, we need to address more directly some questions relating to the nature of that practice.

Action Focus

We have seen previously that a technical cognitive interest evidences itself in action concerned with worthwhile products of the teaching act. For a practitioner whose work is informed by a practical interest, however, the focus of action is not so much upon the products of the learning situation as upon the meaningfulness of the learning experience for the student. Meaningful learning will result in worthwhile outcomes, but products, judged to be worthwhile without reference to the learning experience through which they were produced, do not necessarily guarantee that the experience was meaningful. For instance, entering into a writing process as a meaningful learning experience will result in worthwhile writing outcomes. But the production by a student of a 'good' piece of writing does not mean that the writing experience has necessarily been a meaningful one for that student. Many of the teachers who worked in the projects under discussion provided evidence of a concern with meaning-making in their practice.

Phil, a teacher who participated in the Language Development Project, believed that the very act of being involved in systematically reflecting upon one's work and taking action to change aspects of that practice itself makes education more meaningful:

> Through experimenting with children in a classroom both teacher and students can develop a feeling of learning together

and as a result school work becomes more meaningful in the eyes of the children.

Glenda, a teacher from Martin Valley, believed that the meaningfulness of the educational act was associated with students being personally involved in making 'decisions' about learning in science. Frank, a teacher in the Karrivale project, shared that belief with respect to English teaching, but realized that such actions would be confounded unless there is a correspondence between the overt and the hidden curriculum:

> Classroom activity centred around leading students to independence should be supported by a hidden curriculum that reinforces belief in the students as intelligent people capable of making valuable contributions to the functioning of the classroom.

Yvonne, a teacher from Mount Barden, relates how she confronted the notion of meaning (that is, the purpose of writing) after realizing the inadequacy of an earlier investigation which had centred upon improving the products of her teaching:

> I started out ... confident that I would discover a simple problem with a simple solution, the effectiveness of which would be easy to demonstrate.... Punctuation would be easy to pin-point and measure.

Having identified this area of her practice, or rather the results of that practice, which she wanted to improve, she undertook a number of specific actions aimed at such improvement:

> The understanding of the skills of punctuation, which I felt the children should have grasped in these sessions, didn't produce any dramatic improvement in the way in which children used punctuation.... At this stage ... I moved right away from the problem of punctuation, and looked instead at ways in which I could encourage children to understand the purpose of writing.

Target of Action

It is interesting that when teachers focus upon the meaningfulness of the learning experience for their students it is often their own practices which become the target of strategic action for improvement. We noted in the previous chapter, when discussing the content of a curriculum informed by a practical interest, that Stenhouse (1975) advocated that a process approach to curriculum construction would involve an explication of what teachers might do in the act of teaching, rather than a specification of what students will produce. This concern with improved practice is evident in the work of these teachers.

At Martin Valley High, Pete was concerned to improve the quality of interpersonal relationships in the classroom. This did not involve simply structuring the situation and monitoring the interactions of his students. He realized that his own relationships and interactions with students needed to be carefully monitored as well: 'I have tried to model the behaviour of responding to others by not yelling at, embarrassing or [using] any other method of put-downs to students that are sometimes employed.' He felt that this deliberate effort on his part to monitor and change his practice had a positive effect on student-student interaction. Later, reflecting in an interview upon that experience, he pointed to other areas of improvement in his practice:

> I think it allows me to be diagnostic in terms of what I can do for kids.... The skills I've built up have allowed me virtually now to see kids as individuals and to promote their well-being in a way that I think it should be directed.... It's probably allowed me to be more critical and more confident at the same time.

Notice here the emphasis upon personal judgment ('the way I think it should be directed') and upon 'the good' ('well-being') of the students, both of which are factors indicating a practical interest.

A further example of the need to target personal practice in the process of improving the learning experiences of students is provided by Peter, a teacher in the Karrivale project. The focus of his action was upon improving the effectiveness of group work in his classes, but when he reflected in an interview upon his work in that area it was the improvement in his own practice which he highlighted:

> I learnt a hell of a lot about [group work], because I approached it from a number of angles and I really reassessed them and I learnt not to do things again and now, when I use groups this year, they are far more effective.

A similar concern with practice rather than product is indicated by Mark, another teacher involved in the same project: 'The [project] gave me a more critical attitude. It got me back to where I should have been all the time, namely, changing my teaching more deliberately, thinking about it, planning it and looking back on it critically.' Janice, another teacher in the same project, reiterated in her interview the importance of reflection: 'It's not until you start looking back and reflecting ... [that you realize] that there's a lot there you didn't notice.'

Taken on their own, these comments regarding the importance of concentrating upon personal practice have little meaning. They must be seen in relation to the product concerns of other teachers. It is with great reluctance that many teachers will make their own practice the target for reflection and action. The readiness to acknowledge the relationship between practice and learning, expressed in the above ways, may be taken as further evidence of a practical cognitive interest.

Quality of Action

When teachers work in ways which promote the importance of reflection and judgment-making, their actions seem to have a quality of prudence or wisdom which is different from the qualities of effectiveness and efficiency associated with the technical interest. The teachers whose work we are considering here did not make claims that they were acting prudently, but that quality is, nevertheless, evident in many of their statements. It may be inferred from many of the statements above, so we shall consider here only a few indicators of this trait.

A qualitative change in Angela's practice (a teacher involved in the Language Development Project) is evident in this admission: 'I learned to trust the children and what they prepared for themselves, and, in turn, found them trustwothy. I am now more prepared to take risks with them in all areas.' Mary, a teacher involved in the same project, indicated a similar level of prudence when she began to reflect upon the limits of her prerogative as a teacher: 'I have begun to ask myself such questions as: to what degree can I involve the home and the home background?'

Prudence is borne of such reflection. It develops when teachers are prepared to question their own practice and look beneath the surface of the product to the students for whose well-being the practice exists. Prudence arises when *phronesis*, not *techne* is the ascendant disposition. This entails a transformation of consciousness and a commitment to reflection such as is evident in the following statement from Wendy's report of her work in the Karrivale project:

> That inexperienced teacher described in the opening para-graphs [of this report], who used prediction as a gimmick for getting kids to pay attention, had no knowledge or under-standing of reading theory and insufficient presence of mind to ask herself why the prediction strategy worked.... The teacher's role in guiding the students through to independence in their reading and writing depends largely ... on her know-ledge and understanding of how and why prediction operates as it does.

In Summary

The above quotation aptly sums up the argument which we have been pursuing in this chapter. We have examined the work of teachers involved in curriculum development projects in Britain and Australia and have seen evidence of a practical cognitive interest. In the previous chapter we explored in theoretical terms the importance of judgment and meaning-making when knowledge and action are informed by a practical interest. In this chapter we have seen that these can, indeed, be features of the work of some teachers. When teachers' work ex-hibits such aspects it can be judged as being informed by a practical interest. The significance of these ways of working and the difference this will make to the learning which their students experience will only become apparent when comparisons are made with the ways of working of teachers whose work is informed by a technical interest. The knowledge and action of practitioners whose work is informed by a practical interest are, however, also qualitatively different from practice informed by an emancipatory interest and it is to this interest that we must now turn.

Chapter 6

Curriculum as Praxis

The ways of viewing or doing curriculum which have been our focus to this point have been reasonably mutually exclusive. If a practitioner takes a reproductive view of curriculum which places emphasis upon the pre-specification of the guiding 'idea' and upon the production of educational outcomes which correspond as closely as possible to that *eidos*, it is rather difficult to hold, at the same time, a view of curriculum which centralizes making deliberative judgments and acting to make meaning of the educational enterprise rather than to produce certain pre-specified outcomes. English teachers, for instance, who take a process approach to writing and are concerned that the experience of writing should be a meaningful one for the learner, may find themselves in conflict with seniors who demand that pupils produce a specific number of pieces of work for a term. For these teachers, predetermining what, for how long and how often students will write is incompatible with ensuring that the experience of writing is a meaningful and worthwhile one for students.

The fundamental orientation towards the curriculum which is to be considered in this chapter is that of emancipation. This interest is largely incompatible with the technical interest, but it is compatible with a practical interest. It is, in a sense, a development of the latter. But that does not mean that it is a natural or necessary development. It is not the case that a practitioner operating with a practical orientation to the curriculum would, over time, naturally develop into a practitioner whose work was informed by an emancipatory interest. What is required for the latter rather than the former interest to inform one's practice, is a transformation of consciousness, that is, a transformation in the way in which one perceives and acts in 'the world'.

Although as theoretical constructs the various knowledge-constitutive interests do not sit easily together, in reality it is unlikely that only one interest would dominate a teacher's curriculum practice all the time. What appears to be more often the case is that one interest characterizes a teacher's consciousness and hence will be the predominant determinant of the way in which that teacher constructs his/her professional knowledge. At times, however, it may be strategically appropriate to engage in curriculum practices which appear to be informed by other interests. For instance, a teacher with a critical consciousness might move into a situation in which a technical interest dominates the practices of the school and the aspirations of the students. This teacher might well make the strategic decision that engaging in non-critical interpretative acts of learning is a prerequisite to engaging in critique.

Having said that, however, I would add that the technical interest does seem to be an exclusive world view, with knowledge and practices informed by that interest precluding other, more interpretative world views. Thus, an emphasis upon the educative process, whether that process engenders critical or uncritical meaning-making, will not preclude a concern, at the same time, with the outcome of the practice. The English teacher cited above would obviously be concerned that her students produce high quality pieces of writing. But the meeting of her preconceived ideas of what that product should be is not the point of the writing experience. When an interest in product predominates, however, this tends to exclude, by its very nature, a concern for understanding and meaning-making.

In the previous chapters I spent some time developing the theoretical background of the particular constitutive interest under consideration. In this chapter I shall take as my starting point the work of an educator whose practice is self-consciously informed by an emancipatory interest: the work of the Brazilian educator Paulo Freire. Interestingly, his work has been in the area of adult literacy, an area of education so often construed as a technical operation. Literacy programmes are usually constructed as product-centred; the products of the programme being 'reading' people. Reading is regarded as a *techne* through which other ends are achievable, specifically the production of disposable income through the obtaining of employment by the 'products' of the literacy programme. Quoting Berggren, Bee (1980, p. 47) notes: 'Throughout the diversity of situations the aim of functional literacy remains basically the same; to mobilize, train and educate still insufficiently utilized labourpower to make it more productive.' It is significant that a programme in adult literacy should provide an example of a curriculum informed by an emancipatory interest.

Praxis in Action

It is not my intention here to provide either a detailed description or critique of the work of Paulo Freire. By avoiding critique, however, I do not wish to be interpreted as eulogizing this work. Freire's later work in Guinea-Bissau (Mackie, 1980) indicates that the Brazilian literacy and liberation programme *qua* method was not easily transportable. Freire's ideas and actions do, however, provide a way to an understanding of the emancipatory interest.

Freire's literacy programme embodied three fundamental principles: that the learners should be active participants in the learning programme; that the learning experience should be meaningful to the learner; and that learning should have a critical focus.

'Education', Freire (1972b, p. 45) declared, 'is suffering from narration sickness'. He continued: 'Narration ... turns [the students] into "containers" ... to be filled by the teacher. The more completely he fills the receptacles, the better a teacher he is. The more meekly the receptacles permit themselves to be filled, the better students they are.' Although the metaphors are different, this is a description of the technical interest at work in the curriculum, casting the student in the role of passive recipient of the educational experience. An emancipatory interest, however, engages the student, not simply as an active rather than a passive 'receiver' of knowledge, but rather as an active creator of knowledge along with the teacher.

> Liberating education consists in acts of cognition, not trans-
> ferrals of information. It is a learning situation in which the
> cognizable object (far from being the end of the cognitive act)
> intermediates the cognitive actors — teacher on the one hand
> and students on the other.... The teacher is no longer merely
> the-one-who-teaches, but is himself taught in dialogue with
> the students, who in their turn, while being taught also
> teach.... Men teach each other, mediated by the world, by the
> cognizable objects which in banking education are 'owned' by
> the teacher. (Freire, 1972b, p. 53)

Here is the picture of the students and teacher engaged together as active participants in the construction of knowledge. This transactional view of teaching and learning means that it is no longer adequate to speak simply of teaching without at the same time speaking of learning. Nor is it sensible simply to speak of learning, for liberating education does not deny the act of teaching. Talk of emancipatory pedagogy must, therefore, encompass the teaching-learning act within its meaning.

The corollary of having students as active participants in the construction of learning is that learning becomes meaningful. We must be careful, however, with the notion of 'meaningfulness'. For the majority of the intending teachers with whom I work, their education was a very meaningful experience. The academic curriculum which was 'deposited' in them enabled them to pass their Higher School Certificate examinations and gain entry to a university. Since that education appears to have equipped them well for the competitive academic life at university (by the time I meet them they have survived at least two years of university education), it is difficult to suggest that their experience of schooling was meaningless. Arguing for meaningfulness on such grounds is, however, evidence of a technical interest which ascribes meaning according to outcome, that is, an experience gains meaning through what it produces, rather than being intrinsically meaningful.

In a process of liberating education, meaningfulness is a matter of negotiation between teacher and learner from the outset of the learning experience. So it is that Freire (1972b, p. 65) maintains:

> Thus, the dialogical character of education as the practice of freedom does not begin when the teacher-student meets the student-teachers in a pedagogical situation, but when the former first asks himself what his dialogue with the latter will be about.... For the anti-dialogical banking educator, the question of content simply concerns the programme about which he will discourse to his students; and he answers his own question, by organizing his own programme. For the dialogical, problem-posing teacher-student, the programme content of education is neither a gift nor an imposition ... but rather the organized, systematized, and developed 're-presentation' to individuals of the things about which they want to know more.

Thus the content of the curriculum draws its meaning, not from its ends, but from its beginnings. The substance of the educational experience is a matter of negotiation between teacher and students. (Note that Freire always talks of students, never in the singular.

Liberating education is never a one-to-one learning experience.) The negotiated curriculum is neither haphazard nor spontaneous, however. Rather, it emerges from the systematic reflections of those engaged in the pedagogical act.

Although fundamentally important, active teacher-student engagement through negotiation in the learning situation is not sufficient evidence of an emancipatory interest. Many teachers of early reading have long used the children's words and ideas as the basis of a 'language experience' approach to literacy. Children have learned to read and write through writing and reading their own stories: 'Yesterday we went to the zoo and saw a rhinoceros....' While such an approach makes the task of learning to be literate relevant and meaningful to the students, it is not necessarily emancipatory, for, while it frees the student from the tyranny of text, it does not address the tyranny of lived relationships.

If active participation through negotiation were a sufficient condition for emancipation, then the Ford Teaching Project could have been judged to have been informed by an emancipatory interest. However, the project was not ultimately emancipatory because it lacked a critical focus. A concern with critique would have set the concept and practice of enquiry in a cultural context where it would be recognized as problematic. In the Ford Teaching Project, however, such critique was absent. So it is that we come to the notion in Freire's work of 'critical pedagogy'.

Critical pedagogy goes beyond situating the learning experience within the experience of the learner: it is a process which takes the experiences of both the learner and the teacher and, through dialogue and negotiation, recognizes them both as problematic. This is what Freire calls 'problem-posing' education. Problem-posing education allows, indeed encourages, students and teachers together to confront the real problems of their existence and relationships. This is unlike the 'banking' system of education which, if it is problem-centred at all, addresses pseudo-problems posed by the teacher for the students. The supposition of critical pedagogy is that when students confront the real problems of their existence they will soon also be faced with their own oppression. Freire expresses this confrontation in the following way:

> Students, as they are increasingly faced with problems relating to themselves in the world and with the world, will feel increasingly challenged and obliged to respond to that challenge. Because they apprehend the challenge as interrelated to

other problems within a total context, not as a theoretical question, the resulting comprehension tends to be increasingly critical and thus constantly less alienating. (1972b, p. 54)

Such critique is not simply a matter of being negatively critical about life in general, but rather is a process of discernment. One of the most basic forms of critique is the discernment between the 'natural' and the 'cultural'. This is important because one of the fundamental ways in which ideological oppression operates is to make that which is cultural (and hence in principle susceptible to change) appear natural (and hence unchangeable). Thus, recognizing the problematic nature of existence, it becomes possible to address questions about the root causes of problematic aspects of life and address possibilities of change.

This form of critical pedagogy, unlike traditional pedagogical processes, places control of knowledge (that is, both the production and application of knowledge) with the learning group rather than elsewhere. Hence such a form of pedagogy is inherently liberating. Participating in the act of pedagogy from this critical perspective is to be engaged in a form of praxis. Praxis is the form of action which is the expression of the emancipatory interest, and it is to an understanding of this concept that we must now turn.

The Concept of Praxis

Praxis is a fundamental concept in Freire's work and is fundamental to the emancipatory cognitive interest. Just as we needed previously to explore the nature of *poietike* (making action) and of practical action in order to understand the implications of the technical and practical knowledge-constitutive interests, so also we need to examine the concept of praxis. Let us take as our starting point praxis in Freire's work. The following points emerge in relation to that context:

1   The constitutive elements of praxis are action and reflection. Freire claims: '... men's activity consists of action and reflection: it is praxis ... and as praxis it requires theory to illuminate it. Men's activity is theory and practice; it is reflection and action' (1972b, p. 96). Praxis does not entail a linear relationship between theory and practice in that the former determines the latter; rather it is a reflexive relationship in which each builds upon the other. 'The act of knowing involves a

dialectical movement which goes from action to reflection and from reflection upon action to a new action' (1972a, p. 31).

2 Praxis takes place in the real, not an imaginary or hypothetical world. 'The starting point for organizing the programme content of education or political action must be the present, existential, concrete situation, reflecting the aspirations of the people. Utilizing certain basic contradictions, we must pose this existential, concrete, present situation to the people as a problem which challenges them and requires a response not just at the intellectual level, but at the level of action' (Freire, 1972b, p. 68).

3 This reality in which praxis takes place is the world of interaction: the social or the cultural world. Thus praxis, like practical action, is a form of interaction: 'For the truly humanist educator and the authentic revolutionary, the object of action is the reality to be transformed by them together with other men — not other men themselves' (1972b, p. 66). Praxis means acting with, not upon, others.

4 The world of praxis is the constructed, not the 'natural' world: '... men, as beings of the praxis, differ from animals which are beings of pure activity. Animals do not consider the world; they are immersed in it. In contrast men emerge from the world, objectify it, and in so doing can understand and transform it by their labour' (1972b, p. 96). Thus praxis not only takes place in the constructed world (that is, the world of 'culture'); it is the act of reflectively constructing or reconstructing the social world.

5 Praxis assumes a process of meaning-making, but it is recognized that meaning is socially constructed, not absolute. Freire relates the experience of one of the adult literacy coordinators who presented a photograph of a drunk to a learning group. His intention was to introduce a discussion of alcoholism. Instead, what emerged from the interpretation of the picture was a feeling of identification with the drunk. 'They verbalized the connection between earning low wages, feeling exploited, and getting drunk — getting drunk as a flight from reality, as an attempt to overcome the frustration of inaction as an ultimately self-destructive solution' (1972b, p. 90). If it had been the educator's meaning which had been presented to the group, the opportunity for critical reflection upon the problematical nature of the reality of the participants would

have been missed, and probably with it the opportunity for authentic learning.

Praxis and Emancipation

We need now to make the link back to Habermas' work and the notion of the emancipatory interest. Throughout Freire's writing he refers to 'liberating' education, and so it is clear that his work is informed by an interest in emancipation. We need to ask, however, in what ways Freire's interest in liberation and Habermas' emancipatory interest resemble one another.

In chapter 1 I pointed to the important relationship between speech and freedom in Habermas' work. Habermas argues his case that freedom is a fundamental human interest on the basis that speech, by its very nature, has the principle of freedom implicit within it. Put naively, his argument runs as follows: The act of human speech implies the intention to communicate. Communication implies that the participants are able, at least potentially, to determine the difference between true and false statements. However, since the only defensible definition of truth is that 'on which all agents would agree if they were to discuss all of human experience in absolutely free and uncoerced circumstances for an indefinite period of time' (Geuss, 1981, p. 65), the freedom of human agents is also implied in the act of human speech.[1]

It is significant that Freire also links speech with freedom and regards dialogue as a fundamental human phenomenon. In an almost mystical passage at the beginnig of chapter 3 of *Pedagogy of the Oppressed*, Freire discusses the empowering force of dialogue:

> As we attempt to analyse dialogue as a human phenomenon, we discover something which is the essence of dialogue itself: the word. But the word is more than just an instrument which makes dialogue possible ... there is no true word that is not at the same time a praxis. Thus to speak a true word is to transform the world.... Human existence cannot be silent, nor can it be nourished by false words, but only by true words, with which men transform the world. (1972b, pp. 60, 61)

Elsewhere, Freire speaks of oppression as 'the culture of silence':

> In the culture of silence the masses are 'mute', that is, they are prohibited from creatively taking part in the transformations of their society and therefore prohibited from being. Even if

they can occasionally read and write because they were 'taught' in humanitarian ... literacy campaigns, they are nevertheless alienated from the power responsible for their silence. (1972a, p. 30)

In both the work of Freire and that of Habermas we have the notion of the indissolubility of speech and freedom. Emancipation becomes the act of finding one's voice. And that can occur only in conditions of justice and equality. An emancipatory interest does not, however, either in Freire's work or in Habermas' theories, deny the importance of the 'teacher'. For Freire, the teacher-student has an equal right, given the dialogical character of the pedagogical situation, to introduce his/her own themes into the discourse (1972b, p. 92).

In Habermas' work the problem of bringing 'enlightenment' to others and hence providing the conditions for their emancipation is more problematic. One of the difficulties is that within a complex, post-industrial society communication may be 'systematically distorted' (Habermas, 1970a) by unrecognized interests in power and domination. This will mean that consensual meaning arrived at through group reflection may not represent truth. Understanding this difficulty comes back, in part, to the distinction Freire makes between culture and nature. Empowerment flows from the recognition that the cultural world, unlike the natural world, is a human construction and, hence, is capable of being recreated.

The problem as Habermas sees it is that the distorting power of ideology is such that the distinctions between the cultural and the natural are not easily discernible. It is the trick of ideology to make that which is cultural, and hence in principle susceptible to change, appear natural, and hence not open to change at all. So cultural constructions are represented as natural laws: it is natural that business should be organized to bring profit to those who invest their capital and not those who invest their labour; progress is a natural thing; it is natural that a secondary school day should comprise eight forty-minute periods. To understand what such blurring means for the potential of people to become autonomous agents within society and through education, it behoves us to examine what is meant by the term 'ideology' in this context.

Ideology and the Emancipatory Interest

Debate concerning the nature and function of ideology has become a central feature of Marxist discourse over the last decades. Although this debate has taken its inspiration and authority from the writings of Marx, the exploration of the meanings of Marx's texts has not led to unanimous agreement as to the meaning of ideology.[2] It is not appropriate to this present work to undertake a lengthy and scholastic debate about the meaning of ideology. However, the concept is sufficiently problematic in the literature that my use of the concept may be misunderstood unless I engage in some defining.[3]

Let us explore the notion that 'ideology' means the dominant ideas of a group or culture. By talking of ideology as a set of 'ideas', I am drawing a distinction between what we might call scientifically attested 'facts' and 'opinions' which have not necessarily been subjected to scientific scrutiny. (We will need a return to the distinction between ideology and science.) This is a distinction similar to that which Plato makes in the *Meno* (97D–98A) between 'opinion' (*doxa*) and 'knowledge' (*logos*). So on a fairly simple level to speak of the ideology of a group is to speak of the set of ideas or opinions which dominate the thinking of that group of people. The use of the word 'dominate' here, rather than maybe 'prevail within' or 'are shared by', implies that the concept of ideology has political overtones, that is, that ideology involves the ideas having some power to determine the way in which the members of the group see the world. We might ask: What are these 'ideas' which dominate the thinking of a group?

Much of the debate about ideology has taken as its starting point the often quoted adage of Marx and Engels: 'The ideas of the ruling class are in every epoch the ruling ideas' (cited in Hall, 1982, p. 84). At one level this representation of ideology as a class-based phenomenon draws our attention to the importance of ideology as an element in the construction and maintenance of power; that is, it is those who exercise power in a society, and in Marxist terms that means economic power, who are able to determine how the rest of the society will think about their world. But in another way that is too simple a description, for we all know that the ideas of those holding power in a society, be that political or economic power, are often strongly contested. The so-called Westminster system of parliamentary democracy even builds into its structures the concept of 'opposition'. So an unreflective acceptance of the Marxist aphorism is not so helpful to our understanding.

The distinction which the Italian Marxist Gramsci (1971) draws between political and civil society is useful here. It is the function of political society to exercise 'direct domination through the State and "judicial" government' (1971, p. 12). Since Gramsci was writing under the fascist regime of Mussolini, it was clear how ideology (that is, the ideas around which the political system was structured) could be imposed quite overtly. In civil society, however, certain ideas also predominate; this predominance Gramsci calls 'hegemony'.

Hegemony is not the conscious imposition of the ideas of one group of people upon another. Rather, hegemony is exercised when certain ideas 'deeply saturate the consciousness of a society' (Williams, cited in Apple, 1979, p. 5). Commenting upon the way in which ideology 'works' through hegemony, Apple (1979, p. 5) notes:

> ... hegemony acts to 'saturate' our very consciousness, so that the educational, economic and social world we see and interact with, and the commonsense interpretations we put on it, becomes the world *tout court,* the only world. Hence hegemony refers not to congeries of meaning that reside at the abstract level somewhere at the 'roof of our brain'. Rather it refers to an organized assemblage of meanings and practices, the central, effective and dominant system of meanings, values and actions which are *lived.*

This unreflective operation of hegemony is similar to our 'commonsense' views of the world. In fact, common sense is one way in which Gramsci sees hegemony operating (1971, p. 328). Given this claim that ideology operates through hegemony, it would follow that our commonsense understandings of 'reality' may involve some unrecognized forms of domination. Commonsense views of the world which might mask unequal forms of social relationships may be represented by such statements as the following: The decline of the Australian [British/American] economy is due to excessive wage demands. There must always be a 'boss'. A teacher should aim for individualized instruction in a classroom. I use the phrase 'might mask unequal forms of social relationships' because we recognize, as Gramsci did, the possibility of there being 'good sense' within 'common sense'. What is important is that our common understandings should be subjected to critical scrutiny.

To understand the hegemonic operation of ideology only as being present in our commonsense meanings, however, is to miss another important aspect of the way in which it operates. For it is not simply through the development of consensus over time that our understandings of the world are determined. Rather, it is the operation of a selection process which ensures that certain meanings are those given credence and not others. The development of Women's Studies and, in Australia, Aboriginal Studies reminds us that the way in which we have constructed our educational curricula has given credence to certain sets of experiences and ignored others. Moreover, such selection has occurred according to who had the power to determine the curriculum, rather than as a result of rational processes of selection. Again quoting Williams, Apple (1979, p. 6) notes:

> ... at a philosophical level, at the true level of theory and at the level of the history of various practices, there is a process which I call the *selective tradition* that which, within the terms of the effective dominant culture, is always passed off as 'the tradition', *the* significant past. But always the selectivity is the point; the way in which from the whole possible area of past and present, certain meanings and practices are chosen for emphasis, certain other meanings and practices are neglected and excluded.

It may be argued, however, that such areas of human knowledge as history are always matters of selection and interpretation, and hence open to ideological influence. If we want to escape from ideology, then we must pursue 'science'. Larrain (1979, pp. 172ff) explores the question of the relationship between science and ideology, uncovering the complexity of that dichotomy:

> The relationship between science and ideology cannot be simplified to make them relations of identity ... one should remember that science is not a special sphere of knowledge which may escape from the contradictions of society and the determinations of the economic base; also that ideology is not a simple error of knowledge which can be corrected by true knowledge or criticism. The social determination of scientific knowledge does not make it an ideology, but opens the possibility for ideological penetration.

Habermas (1971) deals with the question of the ideological nature of some forms of modern science. In advanced capitalist societies, he argues, unequal social structures and forms of relationship are legitimized through the technologization of science. Science and technology are fused so that societal decisions are able to be justified as if they were merely 'technical', not 'political' (Larrain, 1979, p. 206). Specifically, empirical-analytic science is informed by a technical constitutive interest in 'technical control over objectified processes' (Habermas, 1972, p. 309).

Thus, although an escape from ideology may be possible through the pursuit of 'science', such an escape is afforded, Habermas believes, through the pursuit of critical social science. 'A critical social science

... is concerned with going beyond the goal [of establishing empirical-ly grounded laws for action] to determine when theoretical statements grasp invariant regularities of social action as such and when they express ideologically frozen relations of dependence that can in princi-ple be transformed' (1972, p. 310).

Here again we have this aspect of ideology being a dominant set of ideas which, in a sense, distorts reality by making that which is culturally constructed appear 'natural'. Culturally constructed ideas are always open to contestation, for they embody contradictions. But when a particular set of meanings which mask the contradictions is unreflectively accepted, and when those meanings are congruent with the interests of the dominant class or group, then ideology is in operation. Furthermore, because ideology operates by 'saturating' our consciousness so that it is embedded in our 'meanings and practices' (Apple, 1979), emancipation from the dominating influence of ideol ogy may not be possible simply through processes of reflection such as those which characterize the practical interest. Thus it is necessary to have some kind of a 'straight edge' by which the insights gained through processes of reflection can be judged. In Habermas' work this is a process of 'ideology critique'.

Ideology Critique and Emancipation

Ideology critique is not simply a theoretical exercise of evaluating the correctness of meanings arrived at through processes of reflection. Since ideology operates through the practices which constitute our lived relations as well as through the ideas which inform our actions, ideology critique is a form of theory/practice mediation. At one level it involves the cognitive evaluation of theoretical propositions, but at another it requires the application of insights through processes of self-reflection. Ultimately it provides a basis for autonomous action. '[Through] the critique of ideology ... information about lawlike connections sets off a process of reflection in the consciousness of those whom the laws are about' (Habermas, 1972, p. 310).

In the mediation of theory and practice, Habermas identifies three functions: 'the formation and extension of critical theorems ... the organization of processes of enlightenment ... and the conduct of the political struggle' (Habermas, 1974, p. 32). A critical theorem is a theoretical reconstruction of the undistorted human competences through which the human species has constituted itself. Put a little more simply, a critical theorem is a theory about fundamental human capacities, undistorted by the operation of ideology, which have been the basis for the species' evolution. Such theorems are not constructions of the human imagination; they are reconstructions from the history of human society, although not necessarily representing the actual history of any one group. This is what makes them theorems rather than history *per se*. Critical theorems are not arbitrary theories about how human society ought to operate. It is important that their credibility is tested according to usual canons of scientific discourse. These undistorted forms of human society which critical theorems posit are only ever potentially present in any particular society. They are, however, implicit in the very nature of human interaction and thus represent a potential for enlightenment and emancipation.[4] Examples of critical theorems are to be found in Marx's critique of political economy (Bernstein, 1979, p. 209), Freud's psychoanalytic theory (Geuss, 1981, p. 74 Habermas, 1972, p. 214) and Habermas' reconstructive theory of communicative competence (Bernstein, 1979, p. 210).

The potential of critical theorems for enlightenment lies in the possibility which they represent for groups to comprehend that there are explanations for the ways in which they are experiencing the world other than the 'natural' explanations which have always been accepted. For instance, critical social theorems may enable a group of teachers to understand that the ways in which education systems are organized are not necessarily those which will distribute education equitably through society. Thus it becomes possible to understand that the ideal of equal educational opportunity for all, which is accepted as being an aspiration influencing the ways in which education is organized and practised, has been 'distorted' by certain unrecognized interests in maintaining the current distribution of power within the society (cf. Connell *et al.*, 1982). Critical theorems do not, however, 'tell' groups of people how the organization or function of that group are in some sense distorted, for they are not theorems about any one group. Rather, through processes of reflection, a group of people may come to affirm that the critical theorem provides them with authentic insights into the interests which determine the organization and operation of the group. This is what is meant by the process of enlightenment. It is the process by which groups critically reflect upon their own experience in the light of critical social theorems.

Emancipation does not follow automatically from enlightenment. Such a view would entail a technical relationship between theory and practice; a relationship which presupposes that once the theory is in place, action automatically follows through skilled application of the theory to the realm of practice. That is not emancipatory, for ultimately it means that theory is more important than practice. There is no freedom in simply following what has been determined theoretically beforehand, even if one ascribes to the particular theory being implemented. Emancipation lies in the possibility of taking action autonomously. That action may be *informed* by certain theoretical insights, but it is not *prescribed* by them. Habermas asserts quite strongly that neither critical theorems nor the insights gained through reflection have any power to determine action, for action in the realm of human affairs involves risks which can only be weighed up by the practitioners themselves. Action following from enlightenment must always be a matter of free choice.

If we return to what was said about praxis involving action and reflection, it becomes apparent that praxis is not simply about doing something and thinking about it. Praxis involves freely choosing to act in ways which are informed by critical social theorems. It is not assumed that because the action is informed by such theorems it will automatically be 'right action'. Such actions must in turn become the subject of reflection, as must also the theorems which informed the action. Theory and practice must both be open to critical scrutiny. Being of this character, praxis is not action which maintains the situation as it presently is; it is action which changes both the world and our understanding of that world. This is what is meant by saying that 'praxis is the act of reflectively constructing or reconstructing the social world.' In this way praxis is informed by an emancipatory interest which would preserve for all groups the freedom to act within their own social situations in ways which enable the participants to be in control of that situation, rather than the ultimate control of their actions residing elsewhere.

Emancipation in this sense is not libertinism. It is reflective, responsible but autonomous action. However, it is not individually autonomous action. Praxis recognizes the indissolubility of individual and collective emancipation and does not promote the individual emancipation at the expense of collective freedom. Thus the emancipatory interest is not simply another form of nineteenth century liberalism which enshrined the principle of private, individual liberty. Liberalism rests upon assumptions of natural law which stress such principles as 'equality of opportunity'. Such constructions of the way in which a society should function to promote the 'good' of its individual members fail to take account of the histories of various social groups. By operating as if each generation were unfettered by its history and could make good if only each person tried hard enough, liberalism has no general emancipatory potential. For groups within society whose history is the experience of collective, though not necessarily individual oppression, liberalism has no emancipatory interest. For instance, although liberalism offers to individual working-class children the possibility of escape from oppression through the possibility of upward social mobility, such individual emancipation depends upon the continuation of unequal social relations for the majority of the working class. Liberalism makes collective emancipation at best problematical and at worst a fiction.

The emancipatory interest recognizes the constraints of history. Through the proposals of critical theorems, groups of persons may come to understand how their history has contributed to their lack of collective autonomy. Furthermore, the critique of ideology provides the possibility for groups to understand that their oppression has not been simply a matter of forceful domination. More often oppression follows from ideological domination through hegemonic meaning structures which mask real relationships of power. The emancipatory interest is an interest in emancipation as a social reality, not an individual achievement.

Thus the emancipatory interest is in empowerment for groups of people to engage in autonomous action. This follows from the development of authentic, critical insights into the basis of the construction of human society by members of such groups.

Curriculum as Praxis

Let us now use these principles of the emancipatory interest to reflect upon what it would mean to have a curriculum which was informed by an emancipatory interest. We have already done that to some extent through our reflections upon Freire's educational work, and we will take up the question through the examination of various examples in the following chapter. For the moment, however, let us draw together some threads from the foregoing discussion and apply that discussion more directly to the subject of the curriculum. An appropriate place to begin is with the concept of praxis: What does it mean to regard the curriculum as a form of praxis?

Some of the constitutive elements of praxis as they emerged from Freire's work, were identified above. Let us examine what meaning these principles have when applied specifically to the subject of curriculum.

The constitutive elements of praxis are action and reflection. If, being committed to engaging in forms of praxis in our lives and work, we were committed to the construction of a curriculum which promoted praxis rather than either production or practice in the Aristotelian sense, this principle would suggest that the curriculum itself develops through the dynamic interaction of action and reflection. That is, the curriculum is not simply a set of plans to be implemented, but rather is constituted through an active process in which planning, acting and evaluating are all reciprocally related and integrated into the process.

Praxis takes place in the real, not the hypothetical world. It follows from this principle that the construction of the curriculum cannot be divorced from the act of 'implementation'. If we regard the curriculum as a social praxis, not a product, then it must be constructed within real, not hypothetical learning situations and with actual, not imaginary students.

Praxis operates in the world of interaction, the social and cultural world. If we apply this principle to the construction of the curriculum, it becomes evident that the curriculum, operating as a form of praxis, cannot simply be about learning 'things'. Rather, learning must be recognized as a social act. This means that the construction of a learning environment as a social, not simply a physical environment, is central to curriculum praxis. Notions of individualized instruction, for long an important ideal of education, become open to critical scrutiny. Such principles do not acknowledge the social nature of learning. If the curriculum is regarded as a form of praxis, then teaching and learning are to be seen as a dialogical relationship between teacher and learner, rather than as an authoritative one.

The world of praxis is the constructed, not the natural world. The application of this principle to curriculum theory entails the recognition that knowledge is a social construction. Through the act of learning, groups of students become active participants in the construction of their own knowledge. This, in turn, obliges participants in the educational situation to engage in critical reflection upon their knowledge to be able to distinguish between that knowledge which pertains to the 'natural' world and that which pertains to the 'cultural'. It is important to recognize that even those aspects of the natural world which are selected to form part of the curriculum themselves present representations and interpretations of the natural world, not necessarily whole 'truths'. Critique of all knowledge is, hence, implicit in curriculum praxis.

Praxis assumes a process of meaning-making which recognizes meaning as a social construction. This principle follows from the previous one. Meaning-making and interpretation are central to all so-called knowledge. Hence a critical orientation to all knowledge is essential when we are engaged in forms of praxis. This, in turn, entails that the curriculum process is inescapably political, for meaning-making also involves conflicting meanings. Those who have the power to control the curriculum are those who have the power to make sure that their meanings are accepted as worthy of transmission. When students and their teachers together challenge this ascendancy by claiming the right to determine meaning themselves, the process of curriculum construction as meaning-making becomes a political act.

Having identified these essential elements of praxis, let us reflect upon some curriculum practices which fall short of being forms of praxis. Specifically I wish to revisit the Race Relations Project and the Ford Teaching Project (discussed in the previous chapter).

It was claimed previously that the Stenhouse Race Relations Project had the practitioner's judgment at its heart. The project was centred in the belief that if teachers and pupils rationally and reflectively investigated the problems associated with race relations, the 'good' in the form of increased racial tolerance would be served. The project, however, lacked a critical focus. At heart the presumption was that race relations depend upon the attitudes of individuals and if each individual 'fixed up' his/her attitudes, then race relations would improve. This approach fails to recognize that race relations are socially, not individually, constructed. What is lacking in the project is any critical social theory that would enable pupils to see the wider social and ideological meaning of race relations.

The Race Relations Project, as we saw previously, was not designed to achieve a pre-specified set of objectives. It rested upon an assumption that groups of teachers and students could rationally investigate their social environment in order to understand it. The project centralized acts of judgment-making on the part of all participants. The approach is summed up in Stenhouse's belief that 'a research on the problems and effects of teaching about race relations should concentrate upon collecting the data which schools will need to support them in the exercising of their judgment' (Stenhouse, 1975, p. 130).

But this is a practical, not an emancipatory interest. Overall the project lacked a critical focus. If the actions of the teachers were directed towards change at all, they were directed towards changing the individual's attitudes. The focus of change was not towards confronting the material conditions through which the student was constituted. This lack of critical perspective was quite deliberate on the part of the project director. The project was a conscious effort to engage in a pedagogical experiment rather than in a theoretical debate (Rudduck and Stenhouse, 1979, p. 105). At least one participating teacher was alienated from the project by this lack of a critical focus (Rudduck and Stenhouse, 1979, p. 85).

Ironically, the pedagogical stance of Strategy A, the neutral chairperson role, has implicit within it many of the features of Habermas' Ideal Speech Situation in which all participants have equal opportunities to engage in dialogue. This freedom is particularly evident in the concern for the distribution of power within the groups and the opportunity afforded to any member of the group to challenge any aspect of the discussion (Rudduck, 1976, pp. 84, 86).

Freedom of speech and opportunity for reflection are not sufficient, however, as conditions for enlightenment in the Habermasian sense. Although the talk was exploratory and reflective, it was not necessarily critical. This lack of critique was not simply an oversight on the part of the participants. May (1981, p. 10) regards this lack of a critical focus as one of the strengths of the Strategy A approach:

> The teachers captured on audio or video-tape their attempts to implement, that is, to test, the hypotheses in practice. And their practice infused with the hypothetical praxis displays issues to the professional audience *without the refraction of social theory*. (emphasis mine)

There is no evidence in the documents of the dissemination of the project of any teacher or class of students taking strategic action directed towards change in the structure or organization of the school or another aspect of their social environment. While freedom is a value stance implicit in the Strategy A pedagogical style, the project was not itself informed by an emancipatory interest.

The Ford Teaching Project was discussed in the previous chapter as being informed by a practical interest. In that project the teachers investigated the meaning of enquiry-based learning in the classroom. At the centre of the project was the desire to 'foster independent learning'. In pursuing this goal teachers used strategies of action and reflection to investigate what it meant to foster independent learning in their classrooms. The concept of 'enabling independent reasoning' (Elliott and Adelman, 1975, p. 12) functions as an ideal in the light of which the teachers exercised judgment to facilitate meaningful learning experiences for their students. There is, however, no evidence in the project's documents of either a logical or ideological critique of this concept. That is, there is no evidence of deliberation concerning the meaning of 'independent' (independent of what or whom?), nor any critique of the contradictions inherent in both the concept and practice of 'independent learning' in schools. This lack of a critical focus meant that while reflection could produce shared meanings, it did not enable the recognition of possible constraints which, by being embedded into the very structure and function of schooling, had the appearance of being 'natural'.

Elliott and Adelman (1975, p. 15) note this lack of critical awareness, but it was apparently not within the facilitatory role they developed to promote such critique:

> One dimension ... not sufficiently picked out by any of the terms used by the teachers ... is the presence or absence of constraints imposed by agencies other than the teacher. In our opinion a lack of awareness of the practical significance of these constraints is one reason why so many have failed to take the innovation process beyond the implementation of informality.

Even though Elliott (1983) is aware of such constraints, they do not represent for him systematic distortions of reality, but rather 'unconscious biases which prevent us from entertaining alternative interpretations'. This suggests that the project was not infused with any critical social theory which would enable teachers to confront or even to recognize the constraints which inhibit their freedom to implement enquiry-based learning fully in their classes. When I say that the project was informed by no critical social theory, I do not mean that it was informed by no social theory at all. The underlying social theory of the project is a form of liberalism which incorporates suppositions about the power of the individual to institute change without a recognition of the historical and social dimensions of the attempt to do so. While schools may espouse respect for individualism and independent learning, the education system acts to constrain teachers in often unrecognized ways from achieving this goal. Thus the hegemonic philosophy of liberalism conceals the operation of other interests which, far from being interests in emancipation, are, in reality, interests in domination.

The interest of this project was, therefore, ultimately practical rather than emancipatory. That is not to say that individual teachers and their students did not find the project stimulating and empowering. The practical interest, however, is ultimately limiting to human action. A similar judgment could be made upon the limits of reflection in this project as Bernstein (1982, p. 841) makes upon the shortcomings of Gadamer's emphasis upon reflection: '[Gadamer] stops short of facing the issue of what is to be done when the polis or community itself is "corrupt" — when there is a breakdown of its *nomos* and of a rational discourse about the norms that ought to govern our practical lives.' It is precisely this difficulty of the practical interest with which the emancipatory interest is concerned. In the following chapter the way in which this interest has expressed itself in the work of a number of teachers will be discussed.

Notes

1 These are complex arguments and it is not appropriate to rehearse them in this present context. The reader is directed to Habermas (1979) *Communication and the Evolution of Society*.
2 Larrain (1979) provides an interesting overview of many aspects of this debate.
3 A reader who wishes to explore the chameleon nature of the concept of ideology in the literature will find the following references useful: Sumner (1979); Althusser (1972); Gramsci (1971); McLennan *et al.* (1978); Johnson (1979); Hall (1982); Mouffe (1979); Habermas (1970a).
4 For more comprehensive discussions of what Habermas means by the concept of a critical theorem see Bernstein (1979); Schmidt (1982); and Geuss (1981).

Chapter 7

Critical Curriculum Practice

When we examined the implications of the technical and practical cognitive interests for curriculum theory, we addressed a number of questions which are traditional to curriculum enquiry: What is the nature of the ideas and dispositions which guide the development of the curriculum? How is the labour of the development process divided? What would we expect to be the nature of the content of the curriculum? How would judgments or decisions about the effectiveness of the curriculum be made? Given the exploration of the emancipatory interest in the previous chapter, it is possible that these traditional questions are themselves a form of masking of some more basic issues for curriculum development: Whose interests do the structures of schooling serve? How can power be distributed more equally throughout the educative process? How can knowledge and action be improved through pedagogical practices?

Moreover, the issues relevant to the examination of a curriculum informed by an emancipatory interest do not lend themselves to definitive statements of procedure. The development of curriculum informed by an emancipatory interest is problematical, and requires reflection and risk-taking action by the participants, rather than academic pronouncements. However, for the sake of symmetry in this work, let me first draw out of what was said in the previous chapter some principles to put alongside the traditional curriculum concerns discussed in earlier chapters.

Curriculum Issues

The Nature of the Eidos

In the previous analysis of the technical and practical knowledge-constitutive interests, the claim was made that a guiding *eidos* of a particular nature can be identified as indicative of that interest. The technical interest is characterized by specific, definable ideas, while the guiding *eidos* which characterizes the practical interest is the much more general ideal of 'the good'. The *eidos* which is associated with the emancipatory interest in some ways falls between these two. This is the *eidos* of 'liberation', a specific good. The idea that freedom is a fundamental human good, attested by the very act of speech itself, has been explored in the previous chapter.

Thus if curriculum praxis is informed by an emancipatory interest, the question constantly to be asked is whether or not the curriculum practices operate to emancipate the participants through the process of learning. Because emancipation will usually be an ideal to be strived towards rather than a fait accompli, we will constantly need to question whether the interest of emancipation is being served, even though our work as teachers within an education system may not issue in the immediate emancipation of our students. Since emancipation is implicit in the act of speech, it behoves us as teachers constantly to be examining the speech going on within the pedagogical situation. The questions to be asked in any such examination concern whether the power to initiate speech and to ask questions in the situation is equally distributed amongst the participants.

Responsibility and Division of Labour

It is clear from Freire's work that the emancipatory interest will mean that not only are the roles of curriculum developer and implementer merged in liberating education, but that the 'teacher-student' contradiction is also resolved:

> Through dialogue the teacher-of-the-students and the students-of-the-teacher cease to exist and a new term emerges: teacher-student with student-teacher. The teacher is no longer merely the one-who-teaches, but one who is himself taught in dialogue with the students, who in their turn, while being taught, also teach (Freire, 1972b, p. 53).

This does not mean that the teacher no longer has any role in the selection of knowledge for study. The character of liberating education is dialogical not monological. This means that the 'teacher-student' has both the right and the responsibility for contributing to curriculum content (Freire, 1972b, p. 92).

An instance of the concept of collaboration in curriculum praxis is the idea of the negotiated curriculum. In Boomer's (1982) work, *Negotiating the Curriculum*, many examples of student decision-making in relation to the form and content of the curriculum are related. Some of these are one-off experiments in negotiation with students. Others, such as the work of Cosgrove, represent systematic attempts to share the power to determine the curriculum, both in terms of content and learning processes, with students. In some of the cases described as instances of negotiating the curriculum, it is clear that what is occurring is merely another name for 'contract learning'. In a sense what occurs is a pseudo-sharing of power, for student decision-making operates only at the level of choice within options. In work such as that of Cosgrove (in Boomer, 1982) and Bertola (whose work we shall examine below), the concern was not simply to provide a wider range of choices for learning, but to share control of the development of learning through sharing theories of learning and curriculum construction with students. In these situations of negotiated learning, students were emancipated from dependence upon the teachers' ability to diagnose appropiate learning experiences. By reflecting upon their own individual and collaborative processes of learning, students were better placed to take control of the construction of their learning.

Efforts to share the teaching/learning process with students in such a way do not always meet with unqualified support from students. We shall see below how Bertola's endeavours to share theory and hence power to determine the curriculum uncovered unexpected ideological resistance from his students to collaborative learning. Cosgrove (1982, pp. 35–6) reports a range of responses by her students to offers to negotiate:

> Firstly, there are those students who are thankful and amazed when they realize that at last they will be able to learn in the way they know they can learn.... Other students view the offer with suspicion, because they don't really think that I will go through with it. They don't trust me. They approve of my attitude, but their experience with teachers allowing them to make decisions about what they will do is not vast. They think that I am 'conning' them.... There are those students who are dismayed at the whole idea, because they cannot understand how they will learn anything if I or someone else does not tell them what to do.... Finally, there are those students who react with contempt. In their opinion I am shirking my responsibility by not giving the class a prescription for learning (the

teacher is expert) and allowing the students to help each other (after all, that's cheating).

Such responses clearly indicate that the notion of incorporating students as collaborators in the labour process of curriculum construction is not necessarily one which will gain immediate acceptance by the students. The traditions of the division of responsibility and the distribution of power in the work of teaching and learning are strongly embedded in the histories of both teachers and learners. We will have many difficulties to overcome if we are to break down those divisions, yet the possibility of autonomous learning demands that we do so.

The Importance of Critique

Two dispositions were judged to be crucial for a curriculum informed by technical and practical constitutive interests. Skill was the central disposition of the technical interest and judgment central for the practical. For the operation of an emancipatory interest, critique is central. Commenting upon the necessity for the development of a 'critical perspective within the educational community', Apple (1970, p. 163) notes:

> ... one of the fundamental conditions of emancipation is the ability to 'see' the actual functionings of institutions in all their positive and negative complexity, to assist others (and to let them assist us) in 'remembering' the possibilities of spontaneity, choice, and more equal models of control.

The idea of a critical community is important here. These are communities of people with mutual concerns, interacting directly with one another (rather than having interaction mediated through representatives) whose relationships are characterized by solidarity and mutual concern. Within such a sense of community, McTaggart and Singh (1986, p. 44) claim, critical reflection is possible:

> Critical reflection involves more than knowledge of one's values and understanding of one's practice. It involves a dialectical criticism of one's own values in a social and historical context in which the values of others are also crucial. Criticism itself is, therefore, a relational concept; criticism can only be conducted in a community where there is determination to learn rationally from each other. The nature of relationships in

terms of power, solidarity, reciprocity and symmetry will be significant issues for critical communities.

When we consider the importance of a critical consciousness to liberating education, it is clear that not only should the teacher have the support of a critical community, but classrooms or learning groups will themselves become critical communities. This will have implications, as McTaggart and Singh (1986) remind us, not only for the tone of the learning group, but also for its organization.

Curriculum Content

The emphasis upon a negotiated curriculum which the emancipatory interest promotes should not be taken to imply that 'anything goes' as far as curriculum content is concerned. It may be true that an emancipatory interest would provide a wider choice for student learning. However, it is also clear that a most important aspect of the curriculum will be the promotion of a critical consciousness. Thus, while traditional forms of knowledge may, within an already established educational system, initially provide a basis for study, the legitimacy of the construction as well as the selection of pieces of knowledge for acquisition must become part of the focus of curriculum enquiry.

Negotiation of the curriculum does not mean that students alone have the sole responsibility for the selection of what will be the focus of study. The teacher and student together 'negotiate' the content. If the teacher has been engaged in processes of critical self-reflection which have promoted enlightenment concerning the operation of power in the learning situation, it would be foolish to suggest that the teacher cannot then make those insights available for critical scrutiny by the students. This is the message of Habermas' (1974) use of the psychoanalytic dialogue as an analogy for the operation of processes of enlightenment. What is important, however (and extremely difficult, given existing structures of power relations between students and teachers embedded in systems of education), is that the possibility for authentic learning by students, rather than coopted agreement, be safeguarded. Habermas (1974, p. 29) suggests that there are sanctions which need to be observed in the operation of processes of enlightenment which safeguard the possibility of the exploitation of the learner. These sanctions are derived by analogy from the delicate power relationship which exists between analyst and client in the psychoanalytic dialogue. Let us examine these sanctions to see what they imply for education.

1 *The fundamental theorems lay claim to truth and this truth must be defensible in accordance with the usual rules of scientific discourse.* For the selection of curriculum content this implies that knowledge selected for investigation must be able to be scrutinized rationally. This also means that the rules of scientific discourse and the social systems which determine what is counted as 'knowledge' themselves become a legitimate part of the curriculum. Thus, while an interpretation of a particular event must be able to stand up to examination according to the 'rules' of interpretation, the rules themselves which determine what we count as valid interpretation must also be made consciously available to scrutiny. Further it must be recognized that such canons as 'rules of interpretation' do not exist independently of communities of scholars which are themselves subject to hegemonic power relations. Opening up the epistemological and social criteria for the construction of knowledge for critical scrutiny must be part of the procedures for the establishment of truth claims. Letting students in on the knowledge construction process is part of what is meant by 'sharing the theory' with students.

2 *The appropriateness of the interpretation, which is theoretically derived and applied to the particular case, requires confirmation in successful self-reflection; truth must converge with authenticity.* When we apply this principle to the selection of content for a curriculum, it reminds us that it is not sufficient for knowledge to be learnt in a cognitive sense; it must also be believed. This is in part the process of making knowledge personal to which Polanyi (1962) refers (that is, coming to have some personal commitment to the knowledge), and it is in part recognizing knowledge as authentically relating to the knower (that is, recognizing that not only is this generally true, but it is also true for me). Ultimately this means that the student is the final authority regarding the authenticity of the knowledge; not the teacher, not the textbook.

The other two sanctions relate more to processes than to content of instruction, but are apposite because the exercising of the previous two fundamental sanctions counts for naught unless they are carried out in an environment in which considerations of the learner as person prevail.

3 *[Practitioners] must comply with the requirements of professional ethics.* For the teacher this means that learning must be recognized as occurring in the ethical dimension. It is not sufficient to concern ourselves

as teachers only with the cognitive needs of our students. Learning must occur in an environment in which the teacher recognizes moral constraint in the extent to which student learning may be coerced.

4   *Within certain limits the [student] retains the option to change [teachers] or to break off the [learning].*   I have paraphrased Habermas' wording away from the language of the analyst/client to that of the pedagogical situation. Neither enlightenment nor emancipation can ever be coercive. If we are serious about the power of the learner to control the learning situation, then it follows that the power to engage or not in the learning situation should reside with the learner. It is perhaps the almost universal lack of freedom in this area of education that marks it out as unfree. This is not to suggest that learning situations should be allowed to become chaotic, with the teacher having no idea whether the student will be opting in or out of learning at a given moment and hence being unable to make any plans at all for the provision of learning opportunities. Negotiation of learning does not entail one partner in the negotiations having no responsibility to the other; nor does it entail a prohibition from breaking off negotiations.

The above principles merely set out some of the theoretical parameters to the debate concerning the content of an emancipatory curriculum. Such principles remind us that questions of what knowledge is to be included in the curriculum cannot be separated from questions about the processes of learning. Educational practitioners and theorists have much more work to do in this area. A plethora of problems — epistemological, social and practical — remain to be solved. Meanwhile, for the practitioner engaged in educational praxis, some possibilities exist for sharing control of curriculum content with students and of ensuring that such content serves emancipatory interests.

The Meaning of Evaluation

It will be clear from much of what has been said above that the emancipatory interest will mean that evaluation is not treated as a separate aspect in the process of curriculum construction. For a start, an emancipatory interest means emancipation from the oppression of external evaluation of practitioners' work. The locus of control for making judgments about the quality and meaningfulness of the work will lie with participants in the learning situation and not elsewhere. 'The participants', of course, include students as well as teachers.

Although evaluation of learning/teaching will not be a separate function, making judgments about the quality of learning is still important.

Evaluation processes which are informed by an emancipatory
interest will not be haphazard. Making judgments about the meaning
of an act of learning and teaching will take place within the
framework of the organization of enlightenment and action within
groups. Groups engaged in emancipatory praxis depend upon the
development of an underlying consensus about meaning as a basis for
collaborative action. Consensus is, in turn, dependent upon the development of symmetrical relationships of power and critical consciousness. Where such critical learning groups are organized, the
consensus developed is not beyond scrutiny. Habermas (1974, p. 18)
sets out some interesting criteria for judgment-making about the
quality of the work of groups in achieving consensus; that is, for
groups engaged in the work of the construction of their own knowledge. These criteria are: the comprehensibility of utterances within the
group; the truth of the propositional components of the group's discourse; the authenticity of the speaking subjects and the correctness
and appropriateness of actions in which the group engages.

'Comprehensibility', he notes, 'must be realized in actuality.' The
members of the group must the able to understand each other. Authenticity relates to the quality of group members' interaction with
one another and can only be judged over time. The question here is
whether members are participating 'in truth or honestly' or whether
they are acting strategically, 'pretending to engage in communicative
action'.

With respect to truth, the key to judgment-making is the rigour
of the critical discourse. There are two possibilities for the acceptance
of the truth of propositional statements within a group. One is that
the acceptance of the truth of a propositional statement is a consequence of the imposition of the truth claim upon the subjects through
the authority of the utterer (be that a more powerful member of the
group or an 'expert' in the field of knowledge of which the proposi-
tion forms a part). The other is that truth has been established through
agreement within the group concerning the validity of the truth claim,
given an understanding of the social and epistemological principles
governing the claim. The latter rather than the former will be indicative of an emancipatory interest. Agreement must be judged always in
relation to the above criteria of 'comprehensibility' or understanding
on the part of all members of the group and 'authenticity' of participation in the discourse of the group.

Similarly, correctness and appropriateness can also only be decided within the discourse of the group. With respect to both truth and correctness/appropriateness, the key is to imagine that things could be otherwise. 'Thus facts are transformed into states which may or may not be the case, and norms are transformed into recommendations and warnings which may be correct or appropriate but also incorrect or inappropriate', Habermas claims (1974, p. 19). This is, in a sense, another aspect of the operation of ideology critique whose function is that of deciding when principles or propositions represent 'natural' truths and when they represent culturally derived meanings which are in principle open to change. A critical community is clearly important for the functioning of an alternative discourse which is necessary for the establishment of consensus about the correctness or appropriateness of actions.

Such principles presuppose, not that evaluation in learning communities informed by an emancipatory interest is no longer applicable, but rather that evaluation itself becomes part of the rigorous meaning-making project of the group. Through processes of self-reflection it will be possible for groups themselves to make some judgment about the extent to which their organization is indicative of enlightenment and emancipation.

Developing Critical Practice

Considerations such as those above represent some of the features which we would expect to find in a curriculum informed by an emancipatory interest. But these are theoretical constructions and their authenticity as critical theorems which may inform actual practice needs to be established. It is all very well to look to Freire's work for inspiration, but that work went on in an educational environment very different from the structured, systemic environments in which most teachers in the developed world find themselves. For us the development of emancipatory curricula is at once easier, in that most of us will not face being put into gaol if our educational praxis offends those in authority, and more difficult in that the sites of struggle are not so clearly identified (the link between literacy and power, for instance, is not so evident). For those who choose to work for improvement from within systems, moreover, there are strict limits to individual or small group potential to initiate change. It would be useful, then, to examine some of the features of the work of some other teachers whose praxis is informed by an emancipatory interest.

In the remainder of this chapter I want to illustrate from the written and spoken comments of a group of teachers some of the features of their work which indicate an emancipatory interest. Some of these teachers were involved in the Karrivale and Investigating Learning in Your Classroom projects outlined at the beginning of chapter 3. I shall also draw upon the account of Cosgrove's work presented in Boomer's *Negotiating the Curriculum* (1982). Patrick Bertola was one of the teachers engaged in the Karrivale project and I will include in this section some references to his work, although we shall meet this work in more detail later in chapter 9.

The questions which I want to address here concern the knowledge and action which would characterize the work of teachers whose practice is informed by an emancipatory interest. In addressing these questions we shall examine the nature of the knowledge with which the teachers were concerned and the relationship of such knowledge to traditional or theoretical knowledge. We shall also look at what the teachers considered to be appropriate action, and at the goals and quality of their action. By addressing the work of these teachers through asking questions concerning knowledge and action rather than traditional curriculum questions such as those addressed in the earlier part of this chapter, I am signifying my belief that in dealing with emancipatory educational praxis we need to be finding other ways of approaching curriculum questions. One of those ways is to cease to focus upon processes of curriculum development as rule-following systems, and concentrate instead upon curriculum construction as a dynamic interaction between members of critical communities.

Knowledge

In the reports of the work of the teachers involved in the various projects which are providing us with a reality touchstone in this investigation, there is a distinction between those who appear to accept the traditional wisdom of their craft (while working to understand it in greater depth and to extend it) and those who question that wisdom. This questioning of the 'accepted wisdom' was in many cases the beginning of a wider critique of the social premises of education. In the work of some teachers, this critique was tentative, no more than a recognition that things may not be as they seem. Others exhibited a more sophisticated critical consciousness. The presence of a critical consciousness is indicative, as we have seen above, of an emancipatory interest. How did this interest show itself in the work of these teachers?

Mike, a teacher in the Investigating Learning Project, examined some aspects of the teaching of mathematics in his classroom. In an interview Mike spoke of the deficiencies he was perceiving through this examination of his own practice in the 'accepted wisdom' that children will learn mathematics by 'moving blocks around and not being rushed'. As his investigations proceeded, however, he began to reflect that finding even meaningful ways for children to engage in mathematics begged questions of the social importance of mathematics. Investigating mathematics raised to consciousness aspects of the education system that had previously been taken for granted. In his reflections upon this experience he remarked:

> The biggest thing that came out of it for me is really probably nothing to do with any form of classroom knowledge at all. The biggest question that I've ended up asking is about mathematics altogether.... It certainly makes things more obvious about what the value systems within education are, what the nature of the obstacles to innovation and reform are.... Maybe sometimes [that] is a little depressing. At least if you've got understanding you're not just floundering around in frustration.

This has become authentic critique because it has arisen out of practical critical insight, not simply as a consequence of theoretical questioning.

The moves from investigating to questioning to critique evident in Mike's perceptions were also evident in the work of some of the teachers in the Karrivale project which had as its basis the intention to improve understanding of the Martin Report on English teaching, and as a consequence of improved understanding to improve practice in line with the recommendations of the report. Some, although by no means all, of the teachers in this project began to develop critical insights which led to serious questioning of the theoretical basis of the document. In an interview Ed made the following observation:

> We uncritically accepted that the Martin Report was a whole and complete statement and, as we found out, it's vastly flawed in a number of ways.... [It's] full of good advice ... [such as] it's important that students come to value the quality of the final product ... and we'd say 'sure, sure, but what does that mean, what do you do about that?'

Here is the beginning of critique. The emphasis is not upon a recognition of the practitioner's inadequacy to 'implement' the ideas being espoused. That form of self-criticism, although warranted perhaps in some instances, is not emancipatory. It only increases the powerlessness of the practitioner. Rather, critique looks back at theory and, while trying to make meaning of it, critically examines its value for practice. Ed expresses a desire for authentic, not authoritative theory. Authenticity is not simply a matter of having a theory that 'works', the demand is for theory which authentically relates to the social milieu of the teaching/learning situation. The development of a critical consciousness in Ed was evident in the fact that he and some of the other teachers were no longer willing to shoulder the blame for not 'implementing' the recommendations of a curriculum report. They became conscious that the theoretical foundation of the report itself had to be subjected to critique.

> It became more and more clear to us that it was little use calling the Karrivale project a scrutiny of the Martin Report, because the more we found out about it, the more we went back to find examples and to illustrate points, the more we found that there was nothing there to pin our thoughts on.... When you come to look at [the report] you find a lot of it is undigested sixties Rogerian liberalism. You know: set the children free and something good's bound to happen. It left out all the pedagogical problems which every English teacher deals with every day.

For criticism of accepted wisdom or sanctioned theory to become critique, however, there must also be some recognition of the way in which the curriculum is both socially constructed and socially constrained. Viv, another teacher involved in the Karrivale project, shows evidence of such a developing critique when writing about some year 10 boys' responses to journal writing:

> Another important consideration is equally broad and necessitates questioning the values of a society in which the fifteen-year-old boy hasn't (usually) been encouraged to see verbal means of problem solving as significant or desirable.

Viv does not take this insight further in her writing, and the critique does not seem very profound until we contrast it with the critical silences of many other of the teachers working in the same and other projects. In the Ford Teaching Project, for instance, none of the teachers questioned whether there was any contradiction between trying to get kids to be systematic problem-solvers in school and the way in which society in general would discourage people from solving their own problems.

Some other teachers from the Karrivale project were more explicit in their expression of a critical consciousness. Peter, for instance, recognized that his relationship with the pupils existed within a social as well as an educational structure. Moreover, he perceived a conflict between the 'accepted wisdom' of the profession (in this case that group work is 'a good thing') and the ideology of the students. In an interview he observed:

> There are a number of ideological conflicts. First of all there is a socio-economic ... conflict here because I teach kids from very high socio-economic backgrounds. I don't come from that background. I come from a very low working-class background.... The second one is that that's reflected in their willingness to work as a group, as a cooperative in a communal situation. Even at the age of thirteen they don't like sharing; they like to compete and achieve.

Peter also recognized that action taken as a consequence of such critical insight is personally demanding and that school structures do not facilitate change by supporting teachers in their critical reflection:

> Ideally we've got to be a critical profession ... we are a very critical profession because a lot of teachers suffer emotionally in their rooms — a lot of teachers have trauma about what they are doing and especially about what they are not doing. But how much time are they given to be able to change?

In an interview Patrick also reflected upon the contradictory nature of his position in the school. His comments mirror some of the concerns implicit in Peter's comments:

> I'm still struggling with the power that I have in my classroom to implement change.... This year I have perhaps had more negative perceptions of the way in which power operates within the school, within the administration, and the relative power of the teacher to create an environment in the school in which the pedagogical concerns are placed above, say, the economic.

The critical consciousness evident here is one which recognizes the problematical nature of the organization of schooling. Supposedly, schools are organized for learning. A critical consciousness, however, recognizes that the emancipatory potential of the teaching/learning situation is constrained by practices which serve other than emancipatory interests. The operation of such interests is not simply a matter to be blamed upon this school. It is not that this school is bad or that the people who have power in the school are evil or self-interested. It is rather that the ideological nature and functions of schooling have a distorting effect upon the pedagogical endeavour. As Patrick noted later in the interview:

> You can't divorce the educational system from a political, economic and social system and if you've got an economic system which is faltering, then the education system makes a good scapegoat. You can't afford to have an education system that works ... it doesn't teach the kids the good values of productivity ... it doesn't give them a hidden curriculum which prepares them for a life of exploitation or exploiting in a social and personal and economic sense.

The sort of knowledge, then, which is consistent with an emancipatory interest is informed, but not determined by, theory. It is critical knowledge, reflectively assimilated and tested for authenticity in the light of both theory and practice. This sort of personal authentic knowledge is acknowledged in the following remark made by Patrick:

> Karrivale was an important benchmark for me; I suppose developing a personal theory of process, into which I could integrate some of the scientifically common sort of theory that I'd learnt in my undergraduate and postgraduate studies.

Patrick's own account of the process of 'becoming critical' is included in chapter 9 below.

Action

Emancipatory action has a different relationship with knowledge from those relationships which we previously saw were indicative of either the technical or the practical interest. When the technical interest predominates, action is regarded as the implementation of knowledge which has been developed in the realm of discourse and is then applied in the realm of practice. The practical interest generates a relationship such that knowledge is reflectively generated through the meaning-making processes of action and this knowledge then informs future action. Emancipatory action is a form of struggle and as such can look to theory for information but not direction. Habermas (1974, p. 33) describes the emancipatory theory/practice relationship in the following way:

> Decisions for the political struggle cannot at the outset be justified theoretically and then carried out organizationally. The sole possible justification at this level is consensus, aimed at in practical discourse, among participants, who, in the consciousness of their common interests and their knowledge of the circumstance, of the predictable consequences and the secondary consequences, are the only ones who can know what risks they are willing to undergo, and with what expectations.

Such action is a form of praxis. Note the elements of praxis which were identified in the previous chapter which are present in this description of the organization of emancipatory action. Action follows from theoretical as well as practical reflection. It is the real, and hence uncertain world of human interaction which is the site for such action, not an idealized or objectified world. This is a sphere which is recognized by the actors as being constructed as a consequence of the risky, tentative actions taken by the participants. In being risk-taking, such action is not irresponsible; it is action which seeks, through reflective praxis, to make meaning of the social situation in the light of authentic insights into the nature of the socially constructed world.

Few of the teachers in the projects under discussion engaged in forms of radical praxis which had as its intention the overthrow of various systems of education. Many, in the light of their improving understandings, took risks in changing individual teaching practices to make their practice more meaningful. Some could be judged as engaging in emancipatory praxis to the extent that their action was undertaken in the light of a developing critical consciousness. The work of two teachers in particular is interesting in this regard.

We noted previously that a concern for the meaningfulness of the educational enterprise is a characteristic of the practical interest. Cosgrove (1982) reflects this concern, but challenges the basis for making education meaningful. For Cosgrove meaningful learning cannot be separated from autonomous learning; as well as the learning experiences themselves being meaningful, the conditions under which learning occurs must be fundamentally changed. This entails the curriculum being a matter for negotiation: 'Negotiating the curriculum ... involves the development of the teacher's understanding of the learning process and of how to provide conditions in which learning can best occur' (Cosgrove, 1982, p. 35). It is not simply the teacher who must improve her understanding of learning theory; she must also understand the material context of learning, being ready to challenge that context if it prohibits her students from becoming autonomous learners. For Cosgrove the practice of negotiating the curriculum 'is not an alternative teaching strategy or a way of breaking the monotony of second term.' It is a means of fostering real learning. The practice of negotiation, however, has political consequences, for it confronts and challenges the very basis of power relationships upon which education traditionally depends (Cosgrove, 1982. p. 46).

Simply allowing students to become active decision-makers in relation to their own practice as learners will not generate praxis within the students unless there is the opportunity for their action also to be theoretically informed. So it is that, as well as sharing decision-making practice with her students, Cosgrove also shared some of her own theoretical understandings with them: 'When I began in my classroom, we discussed the learning process. I asked the students how they wanted to learn in the science classroom and how I could help them' (1981, p. 628). Such action involved risks. The risks were not simply a matter of possible conflict with colleagues who might query the wisdom of sharing decision-making opportunities with students. There were risks with the students themselves. We noted earlier in this chapter that there was a variety of responses by the students to her offers to negotiate. In general, however, it would appear from Cosgrove's writings that her endeavours to bring about changes both in her own praxis and in the organization of that action were generally embraced by her students as providing an opportunity for participation and change. In another paper she reported: 'As part of my research I found out that I spent eighty per cent of my time with boys. I informed them about this and since then they have become interested in checking this and helping me to spend more time with the girls' (1981, p. 629).

Note here the elements of praxis. Action follows upon the generation of authentic knowledge (authentic since it is generated in the light of critical social theorems relating to gender which are authenticated through critical self-reflection upon personal practice). Not all practitioners report such compliance on the part of those with whom they would seek to work in emancipatory ways. In Bertola's account of his experiences (see chapter 9) he acknowledges the possibility of conflict on a number of levels. On the one hand there was the possibility of conflict between his existing practices and those he proposed to begin employing. On the other hand there was potential conflict between the social theory which such practices reflected and the social norms prevalent both within the wider community and within the experiences of students who were to participate in those changes of practice (see below, p. 164):

> If the teacher works towards a sense of community, it might appear difficult to create an atmosphere conducive to the free expression of ideas, the development of a self-concept and respect for others ... when the social context is centred in individual achievement.... The presence of conflict has a further dimension in that students see it as a negative process. They appear to have great difficulty in accepting it as a natural occurrence and understanding that harm comes, not from conflict as such, but from the inability of groups to resolve conflicts....

These insights into the difficulties and risks involved both for himself and for his students in changing established practices so that they would express emancipatory interests arose as he attempted critically to review the practice of group work in his classroom in the light of a developing critical consciousness. As he attempted to share some of the theoretical basis for his own work with his own students, he became pessimistic about the possibilities for emancipation, given his growing understanding of how the students' own ideologically influenced histories were determining their actions and reactions. But engaging in an ongoing form of praxis through which action and reflection are reciprocally related later provided a further basis for optimism. In an interview he commented:

> Some of the readings I've done have given me more hope ... that there's a possibility of ethically engineering the classroom, working constructively on small things which [are] counter-hegemonic in a sense that they attack that ideology, that concretised history, and perhaps make children reflect upon their own history.

Such 'tactics' remind us of Gramsci's (1971) 'wars of position' through which the ground is won little by little. Habermas (1974, p. 32) believes that the conduct of such political struggles requires prudent decisions on the part of the actors. Prudent decisions will mean that one acts, not simply in accord with critical theory, but also in accord with the possibilities of the given situation.

Cosgrove exhibits such prudence when considering the barriers to the change to negotiating the curriculum. Recognizing that negotiation accords with the democratic principle 'that people should have the democratic right to help determine the activities in which they will participate' (1982, p. 46), she nevertheless recognizes the power conflicts inherent in applying such a principle within the hierarchically ordered power relationships of the school (and the society). Taking action to transcend these barriers, thus emancipating classroom practice from the constraints of traditional power relationships, demands prudence on the part of the practitioner. Criticisms by colleagues 'need to be considered carefully and answered by using the theory on which the teaching is based' (Cosgrove, 1982, p. 47).

Prudence is not simply an individual attribute. It is developed in conjunction with others. Sometimes this development occurs through confrontation and the necessity to justify action to others, as in the case of Cosgrove. At other times it develops through the collegial support of others for our actions within groups organized to facilitate enlightenment and action. In circumstances of collaborative action, Bertola believes, it is possible to make some progress in confronting the constraints of ideology upon practice. In an interview he claimed:

> I don't think that [the ideology of the children] necessarily has to be a completely inhibiting factor.... I think if teachers were able to think creatively as a team about what they intended doing ... then I think it may not be inhibiting.

Acting collaboratively cannot replace reflective action, however. The emancipatory interest requires that action, whether individual or collaborative, must always be reflectively generated. Bertola commented upon this essential element of emancipatory praxis in the following way:

> I think the reflexive mode of teaching is particularly important for a teacher to be able to see a progression in their work — to be able to see that things do change, rather than simply going on in a sort of semi-conscious mode of teaching.

In the following chapter I take up the question of how, within a schooling context, teachers might develop the sort of reflective practices to which Bertola refers. For the moment, let us draw together some of the threads of this chapter.

In Summary

I made the claim at the beginning of the chapter that traditional categories for talking about curriculum are not necessarily the most useful when discussing curriculum practices which are informed by an emancipatory interest. For instance, questions which address the nature of the curriculum content cannot be answered apart from questions relating to the power of the various participants in the curriculum process (including teachers and learners) to determine that content. It is not that questions of curriculum content are unimportant; it is rather that questions about power are more pressing. Similarly, if the process of curriculum development is informed by principles of equality, enlightenment and emancipation, it is not so important to decide whether that which was predetermined as an outcome has been achieved, as technical forms of evaluation would lead us to believe. Rather, it becomes important to be able to judge the quality of the learning and decision-making environment and the basis upon which claims to truth are being made. Thus, evaluation does not simply look at the work of learning, but embraces a critique of what is learnt as well as of the interactions which comprise the learning situation. All the time the criteria by which the quality of learning is to be judged are those relating to the degree of autonomy and equality experienced by the members of the learning group. At no time, if the emancipatory interest is informing the action, are those judgments legitimately made by outsiders. It is the members of the learning community themselves who are to judge the validity and authenticity of their learning.

Of course, this is an idealized representation; yet in the work of the teachers represented here we see various aspects of the emancipatory interest in operation. Within the Habermasian theory, enlightenment is reflexively related to action. In the work of these teachers we see that the development of a critical consciousness was an important precondition of emancipatory praxis. I have restricted my examples of the action engaged in to the work of two teachers because of the teachers in the projects which form my examples it is these two, Bertola and Cosgrove, who most explicitly relate in their writing their developing critical consciousness to deliberate actions taken in their classrooms and schools. Other teachers, such as those whose developing critical knowledge was described above, had not, at the time when they were writing of their experiences, moved beyond a form of praxis which expressed itself as a critical consciousness resulting from reflection upon practice. They had not moved to a form of praxis which involved deliberate critical *action*, arising from critical reflection, but directed towards a deliberate reorientation of the power relationships intrinsic to the pedagogical situation. But even to make the judgment that this or that action is emancipatory or otherwise is to assume a power of judgment-making to which another is not entitled. In dealing with this aspect of teachers' practice it is more appropriate to enunciate principles which are informed by critical self-reflection upon practice, and leave the accounts of participants to speak for themselves. I shall thus turn to a consideration of the process of becoming critical, and then leave Bertola to give his own account of his experiences.

Chapter 8

Developing Curriculum Praxis

If the technical, practical and emancipatory interests are fundamental, as Habermas proposes, it is not surprising that we are able to identify instances of these interests in the realm of human interaction. As fundamental human interests, it is also not surprising that instances of curricula informed by one or other of these interests are identifiable in the work of teachers. It is clear from the foregoing discussion, however, that it is the emancipatory interest which is most entirely consistent with the human condition, since the emancipatory interest is identifiable in the intentionality of the act of speech. The question now is whether it is possible consciously to foster the emancipatory interest in the work of curriculum construction. In this chapter I propose that it is possible to do so, and that action research provides an appropriate vehicle for such curriculum practice.

In proposing action research as a process fostering emancipatory curriculum practice, however, I am not wishing to claim that all instances of action research are instances of emancipatory praxis. The fundamental interest in emancipation which is discernible in the history, theory and practice of action research can easily be distorted so that other interests are served. I will, therefore, examine three modes which are discernible in the action research practices of teachers.

When action research operates in an emancipatory mode it is an expression of critical pedagogical practice and so provides us with a framework within which critical consciousness can be developed. Proposing action research as a process for the emancipatory mediation of theory and practice is not to follow Habermas' lead, however. Indeed, he explicitly ruled out 'the fashionable demand for a type of action research' (1974, p.11) as being an appropriate medium for the combination of enlightenment and action. I shall take up this objecttion at the end of the chapter, for it indicates that action research is often understood as a technically or practically informed form of knowledge/action generation. To deny the emancipatory potential of action research is to misunderstand the implications of its participatory philosophy.

Action Research

The action research process is grounded in two essential principles: improvement and involvement (Grundy and Kemmis, 1982). Since it is a form of social research rather than, for instance, physical or historical research, it is arenas of human interaction and practice which form the sites for investigation and improvement. This means that action research is concerned with the improvement of social conditions of existence. Within this process, however, improvement is not to be imposed upon the participants in any situation from 'elsewhere' (to borrow a word from Boomer, 1981) but it is the participants themselves who are to be the controllers of the improvement process.

Improvement is itself a problematical notion within action research methodology. It is recognized that improvement in 'the situation' by the participants is bound up with the participants' understandings of the meaning of that which is currently occurring. Thus, improvement in understanding is inextricably linked with improvement in action. Even the joint focus upon knowledge and action within a particular social site does not adequately cover the concept of improvement, for social interaction takes place within a context which impinges upon the situation and often constrains it in unrecognized ways. If a particular set of social interactions is to be improved, then it is often the case that the social and material contexts within which those interactions occur need also to be improved, and it is always the case that these contexts need to be understood. So it is that action research reflexively interrelates understanding and improvement, knowledge and action, theory and practice.

Simply concentrating upon improvement, however, only identifies action research as yet another change theory and as such does not address the fundamental power relationships implicit in all questions of change and improvement. The principle of involvement is of equal importance with the aim of improvement. Action research is an inherently democratic form of research. This democratic aspect of action research does not arise merely out of a humanistic belief that participation is a 'good thing' or an instrumental view that if participants make their own decisions, change is more likely to result. Such views are at best paternal and at worst manipulative and deceitful. Believing in democratic research because it is either 'nice' or 'efficient' fails to confront and redress the power of the initiator and controller of the research. Such pseudo-democratic forms of research may result in change, but not in emancipation for the participants.

The participatory nature of action research was part of its earliest history, dating back to the work of Kurt Lewin (1946, 1952). Collier (1945, p. 298), one of the early advocates of action research (or research-action as he called it), had this to say in advocating a participatory form of action and research:

> Imperfect action is better for men and societies than perfection in waiting, for the errors wrought by action are cured by new action. And when the people acted upon are themselves made true partners in the actions, and co-discoverers of the corrections of error, then ... in spite of blunders, or even by virtue of them, the vital energies are increased, confidence increases, experience builds towards wisdom, and, most potent of all principles and ideals, deep democracy, slowly wins the field.

This stirring apologia for participatory research and action illustrates that the elements of practitioner control of knowledge and action which have been the basis of much of our discussion through this book are present in the earliest examples and advocacy of action research. Although the participants are the controllers of the process, they are not necessarily the only ones involved. Traditionally, action research has been facilitated by non-practitioners in the situation under investigation. These facilitators may often bring theorems about the social construction of the participants' realities to the notice of the group for reflection. But it is always the knowledge generated from within the action research group which is to be regarded as the authentic and legitimate basis for action, not knowledge from 'outside'.

The principles of participant control are not simply an aspect of the historical development of action research. If we examine statements such as the above, we can see that they are consistent with epistemological principles such as those which are explicated in the work of Habermas. Indeed, it is Habermas' theories which have helped us better to understand the radical implications of the history of action research. This epistemological foundation and the implications of critical theory for action research have been explored in Australia through the work of (amongst others) Kemmis and the

Deakin University Action Research Network (Kemmis, 1980; Grundy and Kemmis, 1982; Brown *et al.*, 1981; Carr and Kemmis, 1986; McTaggart and Singh, 1986) and through my own work on action research and critical pedagogy (Grundy, 1984). In Britain Elliott (1983) has been one who has explored this relationship.

Consensual theories of truth are fundamental to the epistemology underlying the participatory nature of action research. Put simply, consensus theories of truth recognize that within the construction of human knowledge, what we are prepared to count as truth is that which groups of people are prepared to agree is true. If such a view of truth is to have any resemblance to that which we call truth in common language, it becomes clear that agreement must not be a matter of coercion. Consensus must be freely arrived at. Thus truth and freedom become inextricably linked within such an epistemological framework. Similarly and consensus which does not arise from the agreement of equal participants in discourse is a false consensus. Truth, justice and freedom, therefore, all operate together to make consensus, and hence truth, possible. According to Habermas (1970b, 1972), the validity of a consensus theory of truth is attested by the very act of human speech. Speech fundamentally exists, he believes, for the purposes of achieving understanding and agreement. That is, to indulge in a gross oversimplification, the right and obligation to participate in the construction of human knowledge are grounded in the fundamental premises that human speech exists for understanding, that understanding is impossible except in circumstances of freedom and equality and that truth is that to which all people, given conditions of absolute freedom and equality to question and discuss for an indefinite period of time, would agree. These premises about the interrelatedness of truth, justice and freedom establish the epistemological grounds for participatory research and the production of knowledge. The theoretical, as opposed to the historical, grounds for participatory control of action are to be found in explorations of the mediation of theory and practice; that is, in the way in which theory relates to and determines practice.

The analogy which Habermas (1974) uses to explore the way in which theory and practice ought to be mediated is the psychoanalytic dialogue. In the psychoanalytic dialogue, the reconstructions offered by the analyst have no practical implications for the actions of the client unless they are authenticated in his/her self-reflections. Until then they are only theoretical propositions offering theoretical explanations of the basis for the client's discomfort. They have no 'reality' unless the client agrees that they are authentic explanations.

Even then such explanations offer no directions for future action. The psychoanalytic dialogue presupposes that it is only the client who can decide what action will follow from the acceptance of an explanation as authentic. So in action research it is recognized that only the actors in any situation can participate in the risky decisions of human action. The facilitator[1] of the research plays a role analogous to that of the analyst who proposes theorems for reflection but cannot determine the authenticity of his/her proposals for the subject. Certainly the outsider has no brief to instruct the subject about how he or she ought to act. This description constitutes a mere sketch of these epistemological considerations. I have taken up the question of the mediation of theory and practice in educational action research elsewhere (Grundy, 1982).

The Action Research Process

Given that we have identified the action researchers as those who are the participants in the social situation to be investigated, the question is: How are they going to do action research? The pronoun 'they' is used quite deliberately. Action research is not only a participatory form of research; it is also collaborative. Both the history and theory of action research support its collaborative character. Action research grew up along with the group dynamics movement of the 1940s. Moreover, its consensual epistemology means that it is inherently collaborative (Grundy and Kemmis, 1981).

The process of action research consists of a number of 'moments' which are reciprocally related to one another.[2] Given what has been said above about the way in which this method of research relates understanding and action, we would expect that two of these moments would be concerned with developing understanding and carrying out action. These are the strategic moments of *action* and *reflection*. These moments are both retrospectively and prospectively related to each other through two organizational moments: *planning* and *observation*. Reflection and planning take place in the realm of discourse, whereas action and observation belong in the realm of practice. Reflection looks back to previous action through methods of observation which reconstruct practice so that it can be recollected, analyzed and judged at a later time. Reflection also looks forward to future action through the moment of planning, while action is retrospectively informed by reflection through planning. These 'moments' are represented in Figure 3 (after Kemmis and McTaggart, 1982).

	Research (Reconstructive)	Action (Constructive)
Discourse (among participants)	Reflect reconnaissance and evaluation (retrospective on observation, prospective to action)	Plan Constructed action (prospective to action, retrospective on reflection)
Practice (in the social context)	Observe Reconstructed action (prospective to reflection, retrospective on action)	Act Deliberate, strategic action (retrospective guidance from planning prospective to reflection)

Figure 3. Moments of the Action Research Process

This continuous retrospectivity and prospectivity of the action research process means that it is not a linear methodology, beginning with plans and ending with the evaluation of actions taken along the way. It is, rather, a cyclical process in which participants act strategically in the light of developing understandings. So it is that those involved in work of this kind tend to speak of an action research 'spiral' with each cycle leading naturally to the next through the relationship of moments. Discourse and practice (in the one dimension) and construction and reconstruction (in the other) are brought together so that improvements in practice and in understanding can be made systematically, responsively and reflectively. This spiralling aspect of action research is depicted in Figure 4.

Three Modes of Action Research

When action research is organized according to the principles outlined above, it becomes a form of social practice consistent with practices which reflect an emancipatory interest. The emancipatory interest is discernible in the power of the acting subjects to control all aspects of the process and the reciprocal, but not deterministic, relationship between action and reflection. Action taken within the action research spiral both arises out of and allows for the development of authentic insights about the construction of the practices under investigation. When the action research process also embodies reflection in the light of critical theorems, the emancipatory interest becomes even more evident. The possibility then exists for the development of a critical understanding of social interactions and contexts. Such understandings will enable participants to recognize the constraints imposed upon

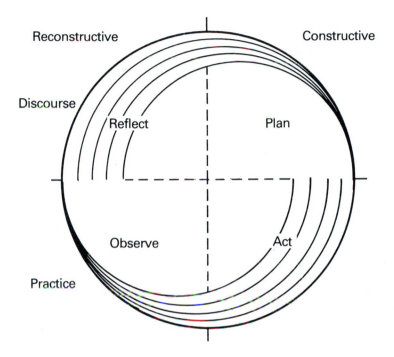

Figure 4. The Action Research Spiral

their practices by social structures and interactions which are informed by interests in domination and control. These understandings will facilitate the recognition that their own social practices, springing from unreflective habit or being sanctioned by the traditions of the social group, also represent and perpetuate unequal social relations.

When such understandings, born of reflection both upon critical theorems of society and upon the immediate social context, are reflexively related to social actions directed towards changing the unfree or unequal relationships existing in the social group, then an emancipatory form of action research may be recognized as being in operation. Emancipatory action research will always be characterized by a critical focus and a willingness to encompass the social context of action within the field of investigation. In this way, emancipatory action research is intrinsically political.

While action research has a coherent method of operation with respect to the activities encompassed by the process, it can operate in three modes, depending upon the cognitive interest by which it is informed. The mode which is fully consistent with the principles of improvement and involvement is the 'emancipatory' mode; but this fundamental interest in emancipation may be distorted by other interests. On the one hand, action research can sometimes be employed as a methodology which coopts the participants in ways which may superficially lead to improvement in their social situation, but which fundamentally makes no change to the power relationships implicit in the social practice. When action research operates in this way it is informed by a technical knowledge-constitutive interest. This means that the knowledge generated out of the investigative and reflective moments of the process is essentially knowledge of how better to control the environment to produce the desired outcomes of the project.

Another interest which may, and most often does, inform action research is a practical interest in meaning-making. This is the Habermasian practical cognitive interest. The practical interest is a fundamental interest in understanding the environment through interaction based upon a consensual interpretation of meaning. It is this interest which informs the majority of British educational action research (Grundy, 1984). The lack of emancipatory potential in practical action research is more difficult to recognize than in the case of technical action research. In the latter it is often clear that the power to determine what will count as legitimate knowledge in the project and to influence what action will be taken lies not so much with the participants as with an outside facilitator or powerful member of the group. In practical action research the problem is more subtle because the participants may not recognize that their meanings are distorted by hegemonic interests in maintaining the status quo.

I shall ground the above argument in some examples, proposing some hypothetical accounts of action research and exploring aspects of each scenario which represent the various knowledge-constitutive interests. Although these scenarios are hypothetical, they have counterparts in the experiences of a number of teachers. The three modes of action research will be identified by means of three scenarios. After each scenario has been described, its features will be discussed in relation to the criteria of 'improvement' and 'involvement' which are the essential features of action research. It will then be possible to discuss the epistemological foundation of each mode, relating it to what we have been saying about action research.

Scenario One

Mr Alpha is a school principal. He wishes to implement an activity-based mathematics programme in line with the recommendations of a new syllabus document. He realizes that such a change will involve more than merely filling each classroom with mathematical materials; it will need a change in the practice of the teachers. Such changes, he also realizes, cannot be implemented all at once but will need to take place over time. Nor will the changes be possible without the cooperation of the teachers. The cyclical and systematic nature of action research suggests to Mr Alpha that this might be a useful method by which to achieve his goal.

His first move is to convince the teachers about the idea (*eidos*) of activity-based mathematics. His own skill (*techne*) as a pedlar of ideas is crucial. His role is not unlike that which Phidias would have played when he first shared his *eidos* of the Parthenon to be built on the Athenian acropolis with his master craftsmen. His task would have been to convince, inspire and obtain a commitment from each artisan to work towards the production of this splendid work of art. Similarly, Mr Alpha must elicit from his teachers a similar commitment to his *eidos*. In doing so, he may need to use skills of group motivation and group dynamics.

Once the teachers have agreed to work towards the goal, the first cycle of planning, taking action, observing and reflecting can be instigated. In this case, the action the teachers take will be 'making' action. Their aim is to produce an activity-based mathematics programme in each classroom. They are to do this in order to implement the directions of the school principal who is concerned with the mandatory requirements of a new syllabus. Such action may require the acquisition and application of new skills on the part of the teachers. These might be skills relating to classroom practices such as the organization and distribution of materials.

Observation and reflection will focus upon the extent to which the intention is being realized. This may involve the monitoring of their organizational skills by the teachers or comparisons of the products of their classrooms with the intentions of the syllabus. The principal, as facilitator of the project, has a vital continuing role in monitoring the implementation, for his is the initial and most complete 'vision' of what is to be achieved.

This is the technical mode of action research; technical because it is informed by a technical cognitive interest, that is, an interest in the product of action. Technical action research embodies the technical relationship between ideas and action discussed in chapter 2 above. The *eidos* which is of a particular thing to be produced (or reproduced), is implemented through the skill (*techne*) of the practitioner which shows itself in productive action (*poietike*).

Much educational and industrial action research takes this form, although it conforms more to the letter than the spirit of action research procedure. That is, it is participatory, but the participants are coopted to work towards a predetermined goal; they do not decide on the goal themselves. They may, of course, modify the goal as they proceed, but they do not essentially have the power to determine what the goal will be. In this form of action research, although methods by which data will be collected or created to provide a basis for evaluation of the outcomes involve the participants, often decisions about the methods and targets of evaluation are also made elsewhere.

This type of action research, like worker consultation, does provide a stimulus for change and that change can be significant both from the perspective of the participants and from that of those viewing the product. Technical action research thus satisfies the improvement aim, but it is essentially improvement in some product and the practices involved only come under scrutiny to the extent that they affect the product. Similarly, improvement in understanding is taken to be an improvement in personal knowledge; that is, the understanding of one's own skills and capacities and of the idea which is being implemented. This fosters the development of craftsmanship. The research group provides a supportive organizational structure in which self-monitoring can be initiated.

There is, however, a chance of manipulation here. The participants may be regarded as the instruments, rather than the agents of change. The relationship between the facilitator and group will then be an 'I — It' relationship (to use Buber's, 1965, phrase) where persons become objects or tools to be utilized in the realization of a goal. Because it is desirable, but not necessary, for participants to be personally committed to the motivating idea, it becomes possible for them to play the 'action research game'. Their actions and deliberations are authentic within the context of the project and designed to achieve the action research goal; but once the 'game' is over, they are no longer obliged to act according to its rules. So our skilful principal might find, if he utilizes technical action research, that he creates a highly effective activity-based maths programme, but that if he leaves the school, the teachers revert to their former styles of teaching.

Scenario Two

A group of teachers believes that it is for the good of their pupils if they (the pupils) learn to reason and work independently of the teacher. Although complete independence is a goal that can never be fully achieved, it should be fostered at every level of education, they believe. Independence, they realize, is an interactive process and its development will depend upon changes occurring in the actions of both teacher and learner.

Action research, they decide, provides a means whereby they can be systematic in their fostering and monitoring of independent learning. Each teacher makes deliberate and strategic changes in his or her own action, but they acknowledge the necessity to reflect collaboratively upon the process. Collaboration is desirable, on the one hand, for mutual support (they recognize that groups function to reinforce decisions to change one's actions) and, on the other, so that they can test their perceptions and insights into their practice against those of others. In this way, a system of shared meanings and interpretations is formed within the group.

Although they are being guided by a fairly nebulous *eidos* of 'independence', they are not creating new knowledge or pursuing an ideal hitherto alien to the teaching profession. Rather, they are seizing upon a principle enshrined in some of the traditions of the profession embodied, for instance, in educational models given such labels as 'Enquiry Teaching' or 'Discovery Learning'. Through their project they give both meaning and substance in action to these concepts.

The form of the action in which these teachers will engage is that of practical action; that is, deliberate, choosing action guided by their personal judgment. Such action is informed by a practical cognitive interest. This practical mode more closely exemplifies the participatory ideal of action research. The impetus to undertake an investigation comes from the teachers themselves. Any persons other than the practitioners who become involved in the project will do so at the behest of the practitioners. The interpretations or probings of an outsider may, however, play a significant part in facilitating meaning-making within the group, but it is the participants themselves who are the ultimate arbiters of meaning.

The principle of improvement relates to social practice rather than to the product of action. Independence is a 'good' to be pursued, rather than a goal to be achieved. Its emergence is not easily measured but is itself a matter of judgment and agreement. Thus, improvement in perception and understanding must go hand in hand with the improvement of the practice itself.

This mode of action research has, as its intention, prudent action within the traditional practices of the profession. Since the goal of independence is enshrined within the values and goals of the profession, critical questioning regarding the contradictions and inconsistencies which such a concept as 'independent learning' raises with respect both to educational goals and practices and to the material conditions which determine the practice of education, does not take place. Improvement will, therefore, most likely occur in individual practice, not in the wider context of that practice.

The level of control of knowledge is also practical. That is, through gaining a hermeneutic understanding of practice which incorporates application along with comprehension and interpretation, personal judgment becomes central to the knowledge process. This contrasts with the degree of control of knowledge in the technical mode which required only personal commitment through comprehension and acknowledgment of external knowledge. In this second mode of action research the practitioner is not merely participating through commitment to the proposals upon which the project proceeded, but is generating his/her own knowledge, and controlling its application through the disposition of *phronesis* (personal judgment).

Scenario Three

A group of practitioners comes to the realization that many of their attempts to foster the good of their pupils are thwarted by the very system which is supposed to be promoting that good. They believe, for instance, that learning requires sustained application and concentration and that if students are to control their own knowledge rather than knowledge being used by others to control them, then they need the opportunity for sustained engagement with learning. Moreover, they believe that learning should be both challenging and integrative. The teachers realize, however, that the system of control of learning and learning time by compartmentalization of subject matter, syllabi requirements, exam systems, timetabling and ringing bells, militates against their pursuit of the good in relation to their pupils. They come to see that the practices and precepts of the profession contain contradictions and distortions. While purporting to promote such goods as independent learning, the organization and constraints of the learning environment actually promote dependence and compliance. Moreover, independence is given a narrow, individualistic meaning which restricts its liberating potential.

These teachers, therefore, decide to examine systematically their own practice, incorporating within that examination both the immediate educational context and the wider social context of that practice. They also realize that any improvement in the area of practice will need to be accompanied by improvement in understanding. Action research, incorporating as it does cycles of action and reflection, presents a systematic way of working towards these improvement goals.

Realizing that they need to improve their understanding of their own practice and the social contradictions which constrain that practice, they engage an outsider who can bring to their attention critical theories which they can test in their own experience for authenticity and against which they can test their emerging insights. This outsider will be like a catalyst in the process — a critical friend, facilitating action and reflection, not directing it.

The action research project will incorporate the same cycle of planning, acting, observing and reflecting moments, but action and reflection will both operate at two levels. Reflection will produce enlightenment with respect to their own practice and also with respect to the wider social context of that practice. A process of ideology critique will, therefore, be incorporated into the reflective moment. Strategic action will be taken to improve personal practice as well as contextual practices which constrain true improvement.

The participatory nature of the project is inspired by more than the two-heads-are-better-than-one principle. It is prompted at the pragmatic level by the principle of the efficacy of collective action in initiating change and by the critical principle of the value of collaborative learning. True insights are a matter of agreement between persons engaged in a learning situation determined by principles of freedom and fairness — that is, a collaborative situation. Because of this, pupils will themselves become participants in the project, not merely the recipients of change.

This action research project will, of necessity, become political. The teachers will engage in 'wars of position' (to use Gramsic's, 1971, phrase) on the fronts of their own practice but also on wider social and political fronts. Improvement will only be achieved if structural change accompanies and enables individual change.

The interest which informs this mode of action research is emancipation; that is, the goal is freedom from the constraints of rules and practices which distort the real interests of the client pupils. This mode seeks to promote emancipatory praxis, but emancipation will remain a prize to inspire the struggle rather than a goal readily achieved. At any one time it is probable that the most that such a project will achieve is the engendering of critical consciousness in the participants, with perhaps only minor 'skirmishes of position' on the action front. But if the project is to mediate between theory and practice, then strategic action must be incorporated into the project along with reflection. In this way both knowledge and action are brought under the control of the practitioners through processes of critique.

It is emancipatory action research that most completely satisfies the conditions elaborated in the first part of this chapter. Emancipatory action research acknowledges the interactive nature of social practice, not regarding a specific occupational practice as in any way separate from the influences of the ideological practices of the society-at-large. It recognizes that liberating changes in practice require concomitant changes in consciousness, but that there is not a linear or causal relationship between enlightenment and action. Rather, they are interactively and cyclically related. Emancipatory action research is participatory in the fullest sense of the term, not merely using participation as a means to an end.

Emancipatory action research mediates between theory and practice through the process of enlightenment. This is the mediating process of Habermas' critical theory. The way in which the mediation of theory and practice in critical theory (Habermas, 1974, p. 32) is given substance in the emancipatoy mode of action research can be summarized as in Figure 5.

The philosophical stances of these three modes of action research can be summarized in the following ways. Technical action research promotes more efficient and effective practice. It is product directed but promotes personal participation by practitioners in the process of improvement. It fosters the disposition characteristic of the artisan within the participating practitioners. Practical action research fosters the development of professionalism by emphasizing the part played by personal judgment in decisions to act for the good of the client. This second mode of action research promotes autonomous, deliberative action — Aristotelian *praxis*. Emancipatory action research promotes emancipatory praxis in the participating practitioners; that is, it promotes a critical consciousness which exhibits itself in political as well as practical action to promote change.

In technical action research the guiding 'idea' need not either be generated by or engage the commitment of the group. It requires only

Critical Theory	Action Research
The formation and extension of *critical theorems*.	Action research does not use theory to justify practice or regard practice as applied theory. Rather there is a reciprocal relationship whereby theory and practice inform each other and are mutually interdependent.
The *organization of enlightenment* in which critical theorems are applied or can be tested in a unique manner by the initiation of processes of reflection carried out within certain groups towards which these processes are directed.	i) Action research employs group processes of reflection in communities of common interest. ii) Enlightenment takes the form of authentic insights into both theory and practice for the practitioner. iii) A facilitator may assist in the organization of enlightenment, but the power to determine truth resides with the practitioners who are the final arbiters of the authenticity of insights gained.
The *organization of action*: the selection of appropriate strategies, the solutions of tactical questions, and the conduct of the political struggle.	i) Action research has as its core strategic action, recognizing the inevitable political nature of social action. ii) Action research recognizes the value and the risk of action and that the only true involvement in action is that of the actors themselves. iii) Action research recognizes the power of collaborative action in initiating social change.

Figure 5. The Mediation of Theory and Practice in Emancipatory Action Research

their consent for its implementation. In both practical and emancipatory action research 'ideas' and actions must engage the group's commitment, not just its consent. The disposition which informs action in technical action research is skill (action is taken as a result of the skill of the practitioners and facilitator in order to realize the 'idea'). In practical action research the central disposition is practical judgment (action is taken on the basis of the accumulated practical wisdom and moral principles of the actor). In emancipatory action research critical intent is the crucial disposition (action is taken on the basis of the interaction between practical judgment and critical theorems).

In technical action research respect for an idea supplies a guiding ethic. In an interpersonal sense it implies a respect for expertise, or, at worst, may represent no more than respect for arguments based on authority. The guiding ethic for practical action research is respect for the autonomy and responsibility of individual persons. In emancipatory action research the guiding ethic extends beyond the individual level to the social. In addition to respect for individuals, symmetrical communication (a requirement of emancipatory action research) pre-supposes a common striving for consensus. True consensus, more-over, is possible only in conditions of equality for participants. The guiding ethic of emancipatory action research, therefore, embodies the social and political ideals of freedom, equality and justice.

Although action research has been categorized by means of these three modes, it may not be that projects can be identified as belonging to one particular mode. These might sometimes be regarded as phases of a project. Some projects may encompass a number of phases, others only one. For example, many professional researchers who wish to encourage action research amongst practitioners begin in the technical phase. The unifying *eidos* is theirs and practitioners are in-vited to take part in the project. If the project is directed primarily by the skill of the researcher/designer and ownership of the guiding idea is not taken up by the actors, the research project will remain in the technical mode. If, however, the participants either take over owner-ship or generate the central issue themselves, the project could become either practical or emancipatory. There is always the danger, however, that if one person's or sub-group's ideas or manipulatory skills become dominant, the project will lapse into the technical mode. It is erroneous to assume that these modes represent developmental stages through which a project will inevitably move. Each mode is informed by a different knowledge-constitutive interest. To move from one mode to another will require the transformation of the project, not merely its development. Such a transformation relates to the consciousness of the participants as well as to the arena of action.

Critical Pedagogy

It is evident from the foregoing analysis that the emancipatory mode of action research incorporates the principles set down by Habermas for the mediation of theory and practice leading to enlightenment and emancipation. It is also evident that action research is a form of pedagogy in which practitioners become students of their own prac-tice. Let us, however, return to the elements of critical pedagogy which we examined in an earlier chapter and relate action research directly to them.

(i) *Critical pedagogy confronts the real problems of ex-istence.* The subject matter of action research is the practitioner's own practice. Furthermore, it is the problems inherent in that practice as identified by the practitioners themselves which are the focus for investigation, not problems identified by outside researchers. There are real, not academic problems. They are also the problems that present themselves to the critical consciousness of the practitioners. Thus, they are to do with the material conditions which constitute and constrain practice, not pseudo-problems associated with the implementation of the collective wisdom of the profession.

(ii) Critical pedagogy involves processes of conscientization. Action research aims at improvement in understanding along with improvement in practice and in the context of the practice. Such understanding does not represent simply an accumulation of knowledge or experience. Rather, it brings enlightenment concerning the real conditions of existence. Thus, critical reflection upon practice generates a transformation of consciousness which is similar to what Freire described as conscientization.

(iii) Critical pedagogy confronts ideological distortion. The way in which action research fulfils this criterion is related both to what has been said about understanding and to the reciprocal relationship between reflection and action. As attempts to modify practice run up against barriers to change, and as practitioners reflect upon their own practice within critical communities, ideological constraints are experienced and recognized. Practitioners will come to realize some of the ways in which the structure within which their practice occurs, as well as the relationships which constitute that practice, are ideologically constrained and constraining.

(iv) Critical pedagogy incorporates action as part of knowing. That this is also true for action research is evident from the above. Action and reflection are dialectically related in the action research spiral. Moreover, it is recognized that practice is the realm in which truth is contested, not the realm of theory.

An Important Objection

Before we believe that the links between action research and critical theory have been securely established, an important objection must be acknowledged. It is that of Habermas himself. In the introduction to *Theory and Practice* (1974, p. 11) he speaks derisively of 'the fashionable demand for a type of "action research", that is, to combine practical enlightenment with research.' This comment is made in the section of the introduction dealing with methodological problems of critical sociology, specifically with regard to measurement. It is, therefore, a comment pertinent to the moment of observation.

Habermas is dealing here with the distinction that critical sociology draws between 'intentional action and behaviour'. 'The paradigm', he claims, 'is no longer observation but the dialogue' (pp. 10, 11) It is in this respect that he rejects action research. His argument is this:

> The ... demand for ... 'action research' ... overlooks that the controlled modification of the field is incompatible with the simultaneous gathering of data in that field ... all operations which can be traced back to the language game of physical measurement ... can be co-ordinated with sense perception ('observations') and a thing-event language in which the observations can be expressed descriptively.... There is no corresponding system of basic measuring operations with which we can co-ordinate ... the understanding of meanings based on observation of signs ... we employ hermeneutics instead of a measurement procedure. (p. 11)

This comment is pertinent to the claim that there are three modes of action research. It would appear that what is being discussed here is a form of technical action research. Although the same term is used, the moment of observation operates differently in the technical mode from the way it operates in practical and emancipatory action research. In the former this moment is concerned with the creation of measurement data; for action will be judged according to criteria of effectiveness and efficiency. These relate to the correspondence of the ensuing products to pre-specified goals. The process of assessment involves measurement. Action research of this mode is subject to the paradox identified by Habermas.

The moment of observation in practical and emancipatory action research, however, serves to preserve elements of the moment of action for later reflection rather than to measure them as they are occurring. Thus, observation converts the event into a text. Perhaps the moment would be more aptly named 'documentation', but the seemingly legitimating language of the empirical sciences has permeated action research language, so that the term 'observation' is common currency. The tranformation of meaning that occurs when applied to the action research methodology must constantly be reiterated.

Observation in practical and emancipatory modes of action research does not result only in quantifiable data (although statistical data may be useful if they can re-create the moment of action). It is more likely to consist of journal entries, audio and video recordings, still photographs or notes; in short, anything which will assist memory in a later reconstruction of action for reflection. This is analogous to the practice of the analysand writing down his/her dreams immediately upon waking when undergoing Freudian or Jungian psychoanalysis. It is not the dreams themselves, but the documented recollections which are the material for later reflection and analysis.

The distinctions which have been drawn between the various modes are, therefore, crucial to the argument that action research instantiates the Habermasian model for the mediation of theory and practice. Moreover, the practice of emancipatory action research addresses the reservation expressed by Bernstein (1979, p. 225) with respect to the practical outworking of Habermas' *eidos*: 'The very idea of practical discourse ... can easily degenerate into a "mere" ideal, unless and until the material conditions required for such discourse are concretely realized and objectively instituted.' It has been my argument here, as it is also the argument of Carr and Kemmis (1986), that the practice of action research provides the material conditions through which the critical discourse of Habermas can be 'concretely realized and objectively instituted'. However, it must also be remembered that action research is not a formulaic methodology which, applied in any situation, will produce emancipatory practice. To regard it thus is to imbue it with a technical interest which, through its interest in control, automatically denies emancipation.

Emancipation will always be the intention of action research which is informed by an interest in autonomous and responsible practice. It is unlikely, however, given the ascendent technical interest in our society, that the emancipatory potential of action research will ever be fully realized in any one situation. Nevertheless, action research offers a programme for strategic action which opens the possibility of working systematically in ways which foster freedom, equality and justice in learning environments and interactions. Action research will not, however, develop its emancipatory potential simply through the application of the methodology. It must be recognized as a pedagogical process in which practitioners critically study their own practice. It is to the writings of one such action researcher, Patrick Bertola, which we will now turn.

Notes

1 In the action research literature the person who works with teachers and other practitioners to 'assist' them in their action research has become known as the 'facilitator'. The traditional role of researcher as someone who researches the practices of others is abolished in action research. In this mode of work, to be a 'researcher', one has to be an 'actor'.
2 We call these various aspects of the action research process 'moments' rather than, for instance, stages, because they are not entirely discrete parts of a process. For instance, while engaged in action one will also be doing on-the-spot planning, observation and reflection, but at that 'moment' it is action which is predominant. Similarly with other 'moments' in the process.

Chapter 9

Becoming Critical: A Personal History by Patrick Bertola

In a previous chapter I referred to the work of some teachers whose practice seemed to be informed by a critical perspective which signalled an emancipatory interest. One of those teachers was Patrick Bertola. In this chapter I include a fuller account of this work written by Patrick himself. At the time of writing about these experiences with action research, Patrick was a secondary English teacher at an élite coeducational private school. He was also one of the teachers associated with the Karrivale project and this writing was initiated through that project. The following is an account of his experiences as he reflectively took action within his classroom to bring about an improvement in the learning of the students. Originally these were two separate pieces of writing,[1] but we have included them both because they illustrate that taking deliberate, strategic action within a learning environment may not immediately result in the positive improvements for which practitioners plan. Initially unrecognized constraints may act to hinder the planned development. Moreover, these constraints may only be understandable in the light of critical theorems about society. Such theorems themselves have no power to suggest appropriate action. Action is always risky.

This is Patrick's story. It is a story in which not only are the cycles of action research and the critical mediation of theory and practice evident, but it is also a story which reflects the hope and despair of emancipatory practice.

All the kids know about groups is that you are with a group of people.

The nature of group work and the problems of implementing it in some social contexts have, for some time, been a problematic area of my teaching; problematic not so much from a lack of theoretical abstraction, but more from the lack of practical teaching experience and tension between my socio-political agenda and that evident in the background of some of my students. Not only, then, was it necessary to begin to explore and reflect on what happened in my classroom during group work, but it was also apparent that this was essential if the theoretical component of my understanding was to have any relevance in my personal development as a practising teacher. It was, therefore, this area of my practice which provided a focus for action research. The action reseach project has led to a heightened awareness of the necessity of cumulative reflection, of the value of programming, and a more practical awareness of the social and administrative dimensions of theory. This latter point includes an understanding of the importance of factors within the school but external to the classroom; factors such as school administration and non-teaching responsibilities. As well, it has meant a realization of the necessary for working through the practical aspects of the theory-practice nexus. As such, this report and reflection is a piece of personal wirting. This is done without apology, for if research and theorizing are incapable of relevance in the domain of personal experience and the microcosm of the classroom (including individual relationships in that context), then that wider concept of knowledge from which we often start our practice and to which we attempt to relate our experience, will have even less relationship to what goes on in our classes than theories of teaching and learning usually do. Of course, an integral part of my research has been the attempt to complete the cycle so that my theory of learning bears some relationship to a wider body of theory.

Objectives which I devised in order to explore these questions were embodied in a three-week programme of poetry study. Generally, these objectives reflected a desire to share my theoretical understandings about learning and about poetry with students and that they would be able to discover some of the practical 'rules' associated with the operation of group work. In retrospect, there was an obvious overplanning and a high set of expectations of what would be possible in the given time. The actual research was certainly less ambitious and reflected, to a better degree, the state of my personal theorizing and knowledge of the practice of group work than my original, rather grandiose, plans had done. I also had to change the research plans because the unit of work was not, as I had expected, based on my own planned teaching programme, but on that of another teacher and in the context of a set structure. In trying to balance my own objectives and the new requirements, my research became, essentially, an exploratory exercise in which I wanted to test the nature, process and value of group work. Reflection on these aspects took the form of some journal writing on my part, written comments by students on aspects of group work, class discussions on the formation of groups and on the extent to which group processes had been utilized, and, finally, interviews with three students. Arrival at this approach was, of itself, an integral part of learning about group work. My understandings of the real constraints of time and administrative demands forced a realization of the limitations upon the scope and extent of research in the sense of its practical operation rather than on the commentary and analysis of data.

My selection of the students to interview reflected, not so much the range of abilities within the class, but more a desire to examine the perceptions of and responses to group work by students at ends of the range in capacity to work in what I considered to be constructive ways in a group situation. Of those interviewed, two were at higher levels of achievement and ability but at opposite ends of the spectrum of success in group work; the other student was of lower ability and one of those in the class who found group work unsatisfactory to the extent that his group did little during the exercise. The members of the class in which the research was conducted were of mixed ability with noticeable concentrations at either end of the range of ability in English studies. They were also my home/form class and this was conducive to a freer atmosphere in the interviews conducted at the conclusion of the research.

In presenting the exercise I distributed a set of assignment sheets and gave a short outline of the requirements for each group. It is obvious from reports in the interviews that even at this point students were beginning to lose touch with the exercise as a result of the assumptions which I was making about their knowledge in respect of group processes. Such a beginning reflected my own conception of intention; the responses of some children indicated either a lack of coincidence of intention or that my assumptions about knowledge had affected the content and quality of my communication.

The first task after students had had time to make personal choices from among the topics offered (in the hope that groups might be formed on the basis of interest), was to make decisions about the constitution of groups. In spite of the request to consider options available and the subsequent discussion, it is apparent that decisions were already being made as to who was to be a member of which group. At one end Mark, already 'categorized' as a problem by his peers and perceived in an unfavourable light by the more improvement oriented of his fellow students, felt constrained to fit in with the members of his group: 'I didn't want to; but I didn't do anything because I knew which group I'd be in. 'Cause I'd been with that group and they wouldn't be working....' Others in the class were prepared to countenance mixed groups, realizing that if groups were organized on a non-friendship basis '... it would probably still work but would take a bit longer as we would have to get used to people.' Underlying the discussion, however, was a very strong element calling for the consideration of marks and achievement by individuals. In the long run, it was this argument which held sway.

The closing of options was also affected by the prior formation of peer groups which reflected groupings of similar intellectual ability. Thus, some understanding of the sociology of one's own classroom is essential if one is to be aware of the social factors impinging upon processes which are seen as desirable. It also highlights the tension between my own intention and vision of group work and those which would possibly derive from the background of the students. The social dimension appears particularly important amongst students to whom acceptance by peers is important.

> I think its a very good idea in theory, but I don't think that there can be a mixing of individuals.... To a certain extent there can be but then you find things like an individual's thoughts, friendships and arguments are all things that affect the group work; once there was some sort of disagreement, well the whole thing won't work .... Because conflict occurs I can't understand why people are put in groups. Individuals vary so much that it is impossible for some people to work together. You have to get on with people — you see your friends in the playground and you take your conflicts into the grounds thus affecting friendships.

It is obvious from discussion that Annette is able to articulate the desirable features of group work, yet considers that personal interests are diametrically opposed to the operation of groups. This may say something about the nature of personal relationships or peer groups and values. It does raise questions about the ideological dimension of the classroom and the nature of classroom operations where there is a conflict of ideology. If the teacher works towards a sense of community, it might appear difficult to create an atmosphere conducive to the free expression of ideas, the development of a self-concept and respect for the rights of others to hold values, when the social context is centred in individual achievement.

The presence of conflict has a further dimension in that students see it as a negative process. They appear to have great difficulty in accepting it as a natural occurrence and understanding that harm comes, not from the conflict as such, but from the inability of groups to resolve conflicts or to move beyond mere self-interest towards some form of empathy.

The presence of qualities of perception, observation and a developing strong self-identity would certainly appear to be linked with the ability to work well in groups as in the case of another interviewee, Vivian, and her immediate friends:

> It's just that I've got set ideas about what learning is and what English is ... I'm very anti-peer group; anyway, some people just do what is expected, but I do what I believe. Group work is what I've formulated over the years.

This clarity of direction and purpose emerged clearly in the way in which the group approached the group work.

> Group work is not as others did, simply saying you do this, you do this, and on the last day we'll staple it together. But Harriet and I read each other's work. It's important to know what each other is doing. Like in our tutorial, Harriet and I changed poets so that we read each other's work and so we helped each other get information.

A positive motivation like this contrasts with the view of Mark who saw group work in a less than favourable light. 'In our class, my point of view is that we don't work in groups .... All the kids know about groups is that you are with a group of people. Just together and you just do certain work of your own — not together.' For this student, getting something done, albeit at the end of the exercise, was an overriding consideration. He was unable to conceive of group work in other than these terms, totally devoid of any sense of joint effort and sharing of all aspects of the exercise. In these conceptions he was certainly not alone.

Very clearly, then, there is something missing in the operation of theory and practice amongst some members of this class. If my assumptions about their knowledge of group work are, as they appear to have been, not based upon what they understood, then there are enormous risks accompanying decisions to work in a new way. This raises a number of, as yet unresolved, dilemmas about how it is that we can share the theory. Other problems associated with my assumptions about understanding of group work were manifest in the inability of most groups to develop imaginative approaches to their activities and to generalize from other areas of English.

It is clear that you cannot assume that children will realize that drafting, for example, would be valuable in the preparation of written and oral group work. Certainly, few came near attempting activities of those like Vivian and her group; such a failure points to the need to ensure that children have an adequate base of knowledge from which to develop their activities. Of course, it also requires some commitment to cooperative effort so that knowledge is pooled in the group and potential activities are explored and developed out of the discussions and deliberations of that communal body.

In order to progress towards such group activities, guidelines in some form are essential. Obviously, many children have not internalized a model of groups:

> People have to be made aware of the ways in which they can work together. People get unsure of what is required of them and I think it worries them — you have to create your own guidelines ... and usually they don't coincide with the boundaries of group work. It's frustrating to do any work without guidelines.

In the absence of any theoretical pegs of a personal nature upon which to hang their activities, such frustration is more than understandable.

Part of the solution to such problems lies in the provision of organizational structures which respond to the needs of the students. Many texts give clear guidelines for the practical functioning of groups, and sharing such theory is possible through aids like charts. Obviously, careful programming is necessary to ensure activities and questions which at least create the opportunities for children to work in groups.

The reference to 'part of the solution' is important for I believe there is a larger problem which as yet remains unanswered. The research has made explicit the contradiction between my values and those apparent in the background of a number of my students and, by extension, individual and group values among those students. The emphasis upon competition and individuality, especially in an acquisitive sense, is difficult to reconcile with my personal theory of the individual and the communal nature of group work. This gap between teacher and student intention raises serious questions about the pedagogical relevance of such activity in the context which I have outlined. Clearly, movement beyond the understanding which arose from this investigation towards a resolution of these tensions will have obvious implications for my personal theorizing and the practical orientation of my teaching.

On 'Becoming Critical'

The notion of reflexivity in teaching is, I believe, central to the development of critical consciousness and the understanding of teaching experiences. Further, it enhances the notion of the teacher as learner through the active practice of moving from theory through practice to further theorizing. Movement away from the idea of teaching as 'once-off' or a series of desperate experiences is crucial, as I discovered in my second formal attempt at action-research. In the action research described above I attempted to examine a number of issues related to group processes in my classroom. The negative conclusions which I drew were, in retrospect, more a reflection of 'truths' half-discovered than of absolute realities. Paradoxically, it has been that process of attempting to synthesize experience and theorizing (both personal and the more abstract variety) which has enabled me to reassess these conclusions; conclusions which otherwise may well have reinforced the negative feelings which I had about teaching generally. The conclusions which I reached after undertaking the first cycle of action research reflected gut feelings and tacit knowings about the distribution of power in my school, and half-formed concepts of ideology and hegemony as they applied in the school and its milieu.

In drawing the conclusions which I did, I was certainly recognizing power, ideology and hegemony as elements which impinged upon my teaching and upon the relationships within the classrooms where I taught. However, they remained as just that: imperfect understandings with little value unless reflected upon and considered from the point of view of other perspectives — made part of an active theorizing process.

What I had concluded was that groups failed to work in my classroom for a number of reasons, the most important of which was the 'contradiction between my values and those apparent in the background of a number of my students ..., I believed that I had perceived an emphasis upon acquisitiveness, personal aggrandizement, and competition. In the context of what I knew about hegemony, I felt that there was little chance of the teacher either exercising power actively to shape his educational world, or to facilitate and effect long-term or fundamental change. Politics and power were reified into all-pervasive forces. I denied my capacity to go outside the experience of my classroom (and the action research) and to think creatively about theory and practice. That is, of course, not to deny the reality of such forces as I perceived. Indeed, the gut response is in turn, I believe, a response to the cynical argument which seeks to deny the teacher the right to act politically. Such arguments represent the views of those who seek to cement the teacher into a political process where 'the functions of schools are antithetical to the aims of education'[2] and where they are expected to become passive 'scapegoats for a floundering economic system'.[3] I had no intention of becoming a functionary, but like the teacher who fails to reflect on experience and simply bows to 'the inevitable' (in the manner of a self-fulfilling prophecy), I had not gone to the next stage of action research: I had failed to reflect, theorize and act on what I had learnt as a result of my theorizing and the theorizing of others.

These issues had not been resolved at the beginning of 1982 when I embarked upon another action research. I did not use the former conclusions as a starting point; rather, I narrowed my focus to the physical structure of the classroom. In spite of this (and possibly as a result of a set of fortuitous circumstances), my considerations eventually returned to the issues as yet unresolved. Perhaps this return says something about the fundamentally political nature of teaching. In order to view my practice from a new perspective which took account of learning in a cumulative sense, I had to 're-discover' that learning was something over which I had power — it certainly could not be delineated by others. As such, 'techniques' like the journal, triangulation,[4] and writing and discussion became personal modes for arriving at another perspective.

My action research evolved out of three sets of reflections rather than as a preconceived programme. The first of these included journal reflections and a map of the classroom; the journal reflections included those made after a rearrangment of the class. The other sets were a paper for my coordinator on a model of joint programming, together with an analysis of attempts at joint programming in Year 10, and a submission to the principal which, in the main, examined curriculum development in the school.

The journal became a prime tool in this reflective process. Previously, I had only used it infrequently, but now I discovered that regular use allowed more questions to be asked of a greater amount of (albeit subjective) data. Indeed, what also emerged was a greater sense of history in relation to my practice. I could more regularly see the sequences of experience informing theorizing and reflection, and thus, in turn, impinging on practice.

In the process of reflection, the use of an observer (a 'critical friend') who was able to provide alternate perceptions and to listen to and comment upon my reflections proved to be invaluable. This struck me most forcefully when it was suggested that I draw a map of my classroom. What was immediately apparent was the gap between what I *knew* in a theoretical sense and what I *knew* about the practicalities of my classroom. I wrote:

> I know the theory of groups. I have a theoretical sense of optimum size, etc.; yet, it has not been until the actual process of articulating the topography of the classroom that the inadequacy of the layout became apparent — [I saw] the value of programming in a physical dimension as well as in an abstracted and process oriented sense.

Discussion with the observer led to a changing of the layout of the seating (including my own 'base') and the location of the blackboard, and further reflection on that altered structure. In this I concluded that there had been some positive change in the quality of interaction and learning taking place in the room.

Of equal significance was the renewed realization that there was some possibility of change, especially in the ideological structure of the classroom, and that there were areas over which I could exercise some power — at least in my classroom. I also realized that my previous action research was, in fact, an act of defining the context of the classroom and my teaching environment. Reassessment of that research and its conclusions about the political nature of my environment was, indeed, an integral part of moving towards a notion of being an active element in shaping the classroom; in this case, by experimentation with its physical structure. The journal (my own and those of students) now became an adjunct through which I was able to reflect on theory into practice and to attempt to inform myself as to what the next step in action might be.

At the same time, I wrote and reflected on the question of the degree of formal assessment which 'appeared' to be expected. Apart from objections to many aspects of assessment practices, and in spite of assurances by the subject coordinator that conventions were nowhere laid down, I still felt a sense of unease, especially in relation to my almost instinctive conformity to what I believed were some of the worst aspects of the culture of English teaching.[5] It was this notion of culture that led me to further reading and the realization that there was a conflict between what I rationally knew about the practice of teaching and learning and the practices 'concretized' into a personal ideology. No one had to lay down the rules — they were there as a result of my own experience. Not only were teaching and learning political acts which one acted out in the classroom, but they were also liberative acts where the actor may come to recognize his history and its potential influence upon his approach to reading and learning.

If I had reassessed part of my practice, then it certainly appeared incumbent that I should attempt to make more sense of the political and ideological aspects of learning and my school environment. In some ways, such a step was assisted by a reshuffle of classes, an occurrence which had its origins in administrative decisions and which led to the loss of my 'target' class towards the end of first term and to major timetable changes. The change provoked some serious consideration of the nature and bases of decision-making in the school and the relative power of the teacher in shaping or helping to shape the school outside his immediate sphere of influence, the classroom. Further, it raised a number of questions about the relationship of economic factors and expediency to what I perceived as the inalienable demands of learning when it came to decision-making. The action research which I embarked upon had as one of its major aims a process which would allow me to make sense of these issues; moreover, it would allow me to look at practical ways of struggling with the forces and their counter-productive outcomes which had existence in an ideological and concrete form.

This was never more clear than when I set to paper my thoughts on a shared programming structure operating among Year 10 teachers at the school. It became apparent that the demand on teacher time operates against any real notion of joint programming, and serves at least two major structural functions: it allows for the operation of a process of maximization of output from productive units in a quasi-economic fashion; further, it effectively prevents teachers engaging in counter-hegemonic activities without a substantial personal cost.[6]

What I also came to realize was that the allocation of power is most often inversely proportional to the amount of classroom teaching engaged in. For example, someone like a bursar exercises considerable power yet has no direct contact with teaching (and may not have had any such experience). This, of course, is the converse of the classroom teacher whose power is restricted to a limited range of operations within his or her classroom. Further, unless administrators add to their burden by maintaining or developing an active interest in learning theory and teaching practice, then their decisions about the operation of a school may well become increasingly distant from the educational demands of the classroom.

These considerations brought me squarely back to the issues which had bedevilled my first action research. In order to focus those thoughts and to move towards theorizing which embodied a set of practical outcomes, I found it useful to examine theoretical material and research which also focused on notions of power distribution and sharing, and the implementation of strategies for change.[7] This pause also served to allow me time to reflect upon, and reconcile, some of the tensions between my subjective experience and theorizing, and the collective experience bound up in pedagogic theory. So as to turn this process of interchange between reflection and theorizing into something concrete, I once again turned to putting ideas into written form.

This written piece took the form of a paper on curriculum within the school and was addressed, in the first instance, to the principal. Through the paper I attempted to place those issues arising out of previous writing into the context of the school and its immediate community, and to posit what I believed were realistic means by which change could be implemented: change which could lead to a more collaborative and liberative learning process in line with the stated values and ethos of the school. In essence, the model called for a devolution of power and the establishment of a process of teacher development which allowed for a reflexive model of in-servicing but which was not in addition to current demands made upon teachers. Whether such efforts have any practical consequences will, of themselves, be a measure of the political process of the school and its willingness to take credence of its constituents in carrying out the business of education.

While I have not been able to address the more general conception of the school as an entity having a political dimension, the reflections have probably raised more questions than they have answered. My practical response to this has been, on the one hand, to return to my classroom with those questions and, in programming, to attempt to provide opportunities in my practice for finding answers to them; on the other hand, I see the action research taking on a more abstract dimension where I can learn more about the school as a setting for a wide range of interactions which bear a relationship to the distribution of power within it.

This could also have a more practical side in that it would give other practical perspectives when attempting to answer questions like: What steps could be taken to develop in-service models appropriate to our learning theory and the history and experience of the school? or, How might the level of consciousness of all elements of the school be raised to the degree where there is a meaningful examination of the question of what sort of school is it that we want? To be able to do this would itself be a political act, for teachers would be saying that they wanted some active part in making sense of their experience, and a role (with power) in shaping their destiny and the development of learning processes and procedures in the school.

For this to occur — for learning to become a collaborative and emancipatory act — I believe that in the context of my school, at least, a number of key issues need to be addressed (not necessarily in the following order):

the political nature of education and change needs to be recognized;

in-servicing will only be meaningful when teachers complete the action-reflection process, translating (or being empowered to translate) their personal theorizing into teaching practice. By extension this also applies to the active function which teachers should play in a democratic process of decision-making in the wider context of the school;

there must be a recognition that power and wealth in traditional social, economic and political terms are just as creative of a restricted view of reality as may be material poverty. If evolutionary change is to begin to occur, then the 'rich' need to be 'liberated';

concepts such as 'hegemony', 'consciousness' and 'ideology' should not be shunned as tools pertaining only to Marxist analysis, but studied and recognized as factors which have an important bearing on what goes on in institutionalized learning;

change might come more easily if we recognized the need, in teaching, to do less more thoroughly rather than attempting to do too much by halves.

While these points may seem self-evident, I believe that until they become part of the continuing reflexive process of the teacher, their implications will not be fully explored by those at the heart of the practice of teaching: our tacit knowings or those things to which we say 'I know that already', will only then become meaningful in making sense of our experience, and be a positive element in an expanding and comprehensive process of theorizing about that experience.

Notes

1 An earlier version of the paper 'Becoming critical: A personal history', was published in *Interpretations* the Journal of the Western Australian English Teachers' Association. We gratefully acknowledge permission of the editor to include the paper in this chapter.
2 David Homer (1982) 'English and the electronic media', in *English in Australia*, 60 (June), p. 38.
3 *Ibid.*
4 Triangulation is a technique used extensively in the Ford Teaching Project (see chapter 5 above) for cross-checking interpretations of an event.
5 At numerous staff meetings there had also been 'apparent' agreement on the fact of overassessment.
6 Those actions which seek to promote resistance to oppressive structures and processes and provide a focus for action for constructive (and participatory) change. For further discussion see Henry A. Giroux (1981) 'Hegemony, resistance, and the paradox of educational reform', in *Interchange*, 12, 2–3, pp. 3–26.
7 R.D. Eagleson (Ed.) (1982) *English in the Eighties*, Adelaide, AATE; Henry A. Giroux (1980) 'Beyond the limits of radical educational reform: Towards a critical theory of education', in *Journal of Curriculum Theorizing*, 2, 1, pp. 20–46; James Moffett (1981) *Coming on Center: English Education in Evolution*, Montclair, Boynton/Cook; David Pettit (1980) *Opening up Schools: Schools and Community in Australia*, Ringwood, Penguin; Schools' Commission (1980) *Schooling for 15 and 16 Year-Olds*, Canberra, AGPS.

Chapter 10

Curriculum Praxis and Teachers' Work

> It has always been a great temptation, for men of action no less than for men of thought, to find a substitute for action in the hope that the realm of human affairs may escape the hapha-zardness and moral irresponsibility inherent in a plurality of agents. (Arendt, 1958)

Teachers work in the haphazard realm of human affairs of which Arendt speaks. Within the 'plurality of agents' which makes up the classroom and the school, the tendency to find a substitute for action in the hope of escaping the haphazardness of the education enterprise has been strong. This is the tendency towards substituting behaviour for action. It is a tendency encouraged by the technical interest which permeates so much of our lives and work. There is, however, another tendency with respect to human action which proves to be almost as problematic. This is the tendency to engage in the risky domain of human action, but to be guided in judgments about action by an interpretation of the meaning of the situation which is constrained by traditional meanings. Such action is an outworking of a practical interest in understanding and meaningful action. The problem is to act in ways which are not already predetermined by habitual practice. Arendt's work in investigating 'the human condition' (1958, p. 220) would propose that 'action' which proceeds from judgment-making is a more authentic form of human endeavour than rule-generating or rule-following 'behaviour'. Habermas' distinction between the prac-tical and emancipatory interests suggests to us that there are yet other possibilities for human action, and hence for occupational practice.

In this final chapter I shall explore what the various theoretical constructs which are encapsulated in the theory of cognitive interests mean with respect to the nature of teachers' work. Firstly I shall explore the nature of teachers' work when it is constructed as an attempt to escape the haphazard realm by constituting itself as productive action. I shall then consider what it means for the nature of that work when the uncertainties of classroom life are accepted and embraced and practical action ensues. I will argue further that this does not exhaust the possibilities for the ways in which teachers might work. Something else is needed if teachers' work is to realize the potential it has for promoting autonomous and responsible learning. What is needed is neither an escape from nor an embracing of uncertainty. Rather, there is a need for a mode of work which acknowledges the possibility of distinguishing between areas of curriculum practice in which it is appropriate either to 'work to rule' or to exercise judgment, and those in which unrecognized interests in domination transform the latter into the former. This is a form of emancipatory praxis.

These are not new or unfamiliar ways of working. The implication of the theory of cognitive interests is that teachers' work may be constructed in a variety of forms. When their work is informed by a technical interest, I shall argue that teachers engage in a form of work which is characterized by 'craftsmanship'.[1] When judgment is the predominant disposition which informs teachers' work, their work may be judged to be informed by 'professionalism'. One of the implications of the theories which we have been discussing here, however, is that there exists the possibility for teachers' work (and for that matter the work of those engaged in other occupations) to move beyond professionalism. I have called the disposition which informs people's work in these circumstances the disposition of 'practique' (Grundy, 1984).

Technical and Practical Action Revisited

To explore teachers' work in this way, we need to revisit some of the notions about human action introduced in earlier chapters. It follows from our earlier explorations that practical action (Aristotelian *praxis*) is the characteristic human action associated with the haphazard realm in which judgment is demanded, and that productive action (*poiesis*) is associated with the technical realm in which the skilful application of rules of procedure provides the basis for action.

We have seen previously that Aristotle makes this distinction between *poietike* (making) and *praxis* (doing) in Book VI of the *Nicomachean Ethics* (1140a, 6). Productive action follows from the human disposition *techne* (skill) and we would call it 'technical' action. It is this technical action which Habermas calls 'purposive-rational action' (1971, p. 91). Practical action, on the other hand, is reliant upon the human disposition of *phronesis* (practical judgment).

We have also seen that *phronesis* is a complex term and no English word is capable of capturing the range of meanings implicit in the original Greek. *Phronesis* is the basis of the prudence of the magistrate whose discretion indicates when to apply and when to refrain from the application of the full rigour of the law. *Phronesis* also involves taste.

> [Taste] constitutes a special way of knowing. It belongs in the area of ... reflective judgment .... Both taste and judgment are evaluations of the object in relation to the whole to see if it fits in with everything else, whether, then, it is 'fitting'. (Gadamer, 1979, p. 36).

Practical judgment involves prudence as well as knowledge and the taking account of what is fitting as well as of what is right.

Purposive rational action ('making' action) is product oriented and teleological in nature. Its success depends upon the transformation of the originating idea into action through the mediation of the operator's skill. Practical action is ontological; that is, it engages the person who is taking the action in existential choice. For practical action the nature and quality of the action itself are more important than what is produced as an outcome. The emphasis is thus placed upon taking action (the doing) which is guided by a moral *eidos* ('the good') and mediated through the practical judgment of the actor.

Purposive-Rational Action

Aristotle, like his predecessors, included art, craft and applied science under the term *poietike* (Aristotle, *Nic. Ethics*, V1, 1140a, 1–20), but the term is too diffuse to encompass adequately all modern categories of product oriented occupations. Habermas distinguishes two categories of purposive-rational action: instrumental and strategic action. His distinction is worth quoting at length.

> Instrumental action is governed by technical rules based on empirical knowledge. In every case they imply conditional predictions about observable events, physical or social. These predictions can prove correct or incorrect. The conduct of

rational choices is governed by strategies based on analytical knowledge. They imply deductions from preference rules (value systems) and decision procedures; these dispositions are either correctly or incorrectly deduced ... while instrumental action organizes means that are appropriate or inappropriate according to criteria of an effective control of reality, strategic action depends only on the correct evaluation of possible alternative choices, which results from calculation supplemented by values and maxims. (Habermas, 1971, pp. 91–2).

The value of this distinction, in McCarthy's (1978, p. 24) view, is that it allows a separation to be made between technical progress as such and decision-making procedures. But McCarthy further believes that it is a mistake to think of them as two types of action. Rather, they should be seen as two moments of purposive-rational action. This is important because certain actions often appear to require judgment-making, but if we enquire about the nature of the judgments being made, we find that they are strategic, not practical. It seems often to be the case that research into problem-solving has this strategic intention. That is, the intention of the research is to identify the processes by which decisions are made in order to provide sets of procedures for decision-making. Decision-making, then, becomes yet another form of rule-following.

This distinction between instrumental and strategic action can be illustrated by exploring the rather fine distinction between 'workmanship' and 'craftsmanship'. In common language we distinguish between those artefacts that are characterized by workmanship and those that are characterized by craftsmanship. The latter has more of the 'person' of the artisan in it. It is as if craftsmanship engaged the worker's commitment (Polanyi, 1962, p. 61) as well as his/her skill. On the other hand, it is the high degree of skill which is admired when we acknowledge the workmanship of an artefact. Craftsmanship is mediated through judgment as well as through skill, while workmanship relies prodominantly, if not entirely, upon skill. Workmanship is the character of work required when the activity is essentially reproductive, while craftsmanship characterizes productive labour. Both being forms of purposive-rational action, they are constituted through an interest in 'the possible securing and expansion, through information, of feed-back monitored action. This is the cognitive interest in technical control over objectified processes' (Habermas, 1972, p. 309).

These notions of instrumental and strategic action are important in understanding the work of teachers as mediators of the curriculum. There has been a strong reaction in recent curriculum theory (though not necessarily in curriculum practice) against an instrumental view of teachers' work (for example, Stenhouse, 1975; Apple, 1979). This is a reaction against the view that teachers are simply technicians who take that which is designed and developed elsewhere and apply it in educational settings. Since Schwab (1969) published his seminal papers advocating the reinstatement of teachers' judgment and the arts of deliberation as the central motifs of curriculum processes, there has been an acknowledgment that deliberation is an important element in curriculum decision-making. The shift has been deceptive, however, for the change has often resulted in strategic rather than practical decision-making; that is, choice has been exercised within a predetermined system of options or according to decision-making procedures oriented towards the production of previously determined, desirable educational outcomes.

An example of this tendency towards the technologization of deliberation and judgment-making is provided by the application of the Nominal Group Technique (Hegarty, 1977; O'Neil, 1981) in the area of curriculum decision-making. This technique has become popular with curriculum consultants as a means of identifying areas of concern and action priorities. Although the participating groups in any such exercise are engaged in decision-making, the process is controlled by the application of the technique. The procedure is deemed to be more successful the more closely the steps of the technique are adhered to. The technique itself guarantees that an outcome of consensus will be achieved. The rules of procedure assist the participants to escape the haphazardness inherent in a situation involving a plurality of agents. Although there is no denying that the participants are engaged in making judgments, the judgments are strategic, not personal. This is decision-making which is informed by a technical interest. The curriculum consultant who adopts such a form of decision-making is engaging in a mode of work which has the characteristics of a craft. Through the exercising of his/her skill in applying the technique, a set of action priorities is produced.

We can see this tendency towards craftsmanship in the act of teaching in other areas as well. Turney *et al.* (1986) have analyzed the work of teaching in terms of the diversity of roles which a teacher takes on in the teaching and learning environment. This analysis constructs teaching as a craft. While it is always acknowledged that the skills of teaching are high-level skills, requiring a high level of personal commitment, it is, nevertheless, a skills-based approach to teaching. The very notion that all the aspects of a teacher's work can be identified and named suggests that this is a craft which can be mastered.

This is not to suggest that such an analysis of teachers' work has no merit. Turney and his team have done teacher education a service by identifying areas of practice, the systematic monitoring of which has the potential to improve the educational experiences of learners. The problem is that a technical interest suggests that such teaching practices as questioning strategies are important because they are an essential part of the repertoire of skills possessed by a teacher. Questioning skilfully is part of what a teacher must do in order to produce desirable educational outcomes.

There are, however, other ways of approaching the use of questions by teachers. On the one hand, teachers' questioning practices may be regarded as the means by which learning is made meaningful, and meaningfulness is monitored. In this case, the choice of which question to ask becomes a matter of personal judgment, not a matter of skill or strategic decision-making. At another level, however, the asking of questions can be recognized as a fundamental way in which power is both maintained and distributed in a learning situation. In this case, to exercise one's skill in questioning is to exercise control of the learning environment and the learners. To work in a way which distributes power equitably in the learning environment is to adopt an approach to questioning which not only recognizes the importance of judgment, but also the importance of negotiation and symmetry in the discourse of learning. To work in either of these last two ways is to move beyond craftsmanship.

Professional Practice

When the work of teachers is informed by a technical interest, the work is recognizable as a manifestation of craftsmanship (or perhaps workmanship). When the practices which foster learning are engaged in a way which is dependent upon the exercising of the practitioner's practical judgments, then that work may be deemed to be characterized by professionalism. Professionalism has its outcome in 'practical action'.

We have seen previously that, while 'making' action is informed by a technical cognitive interest (that is, an interest in manipulation and control), practical action (Aristotelian *praxis*) is informed by a practical interest. As we have seen before, to the Greeks the practical life was not the production of artefacts or the management of business affairs, but the life of the *polis*, that is, the interactive, political life.[2] It is in the interactive arena that *phronesis* (practical judgment) is exercised. Aristotle declared: 'Practical judgment (*phronesis*) ... is concerned with human affairs and with matters about which deliberation is possible' (*Nic. Ethics*, 1141b). The process of deliberation in which *phronesis* is involved is informed by a practical cognitive interest, that is, 'an interest that has as its aim not technical control or manipulation, but the clarifying of the conditions of communication and intersubjectivity' (Bernstein, 1979, p. 197).

Phronesis, it has been noted before, has its action outcome in a form of *praxis*, what Habermas calls 'communicative action' or 'symbolic interaction'. 'Statements about the object domain of persons and utterances ... can only be retranslated into orientations governing communicative action' (1972, p. 370). His explanation of this type of human action is given in *Towards a Rational Society*:

> By 'interaction' ... I understand communicative action, symbolic interaction. It is governed by binding consensual norms, which define reciprocal expectations about behaviour and which must be understood and recognized by at least two acting subjects. Social norms are enforced through sanctions.... While the validity of technical rules and strategies depends on that of empirically true or analytically correct propositions, the validity of social norms is grounded only in the inter-subjectivity of the mutual understanding of intentions secured by the general recognition of obligations. (1971, p. 92)

The relationship here between knowledge and action is not direct; rather it is dependent upon deliberation, shared understanding and intention. The same deliberative relationship existed for Aristotle between *phronesis* and action:

> Since moral virtue is a characteristic involving choice, and since choice is a deliberate desire, it follows that, if the choice is to be good, the reasoning must be true and the desire correct.... This, then, is the kind of thought and the kind of truth that is practical and concerned with action (*praxis*). (*Nic. Ethics*, V1, 1139a)

Here we see the importance of choice, but not strategic choice between pre-specified alternatives as in strategic action. Rather, this is choice from a much wider set of alternatives; alternatives which arise out of open processes of deliberation.

In Book III of this same work Aristotle emphasizes the inter-subjective and mediatory nature of deliberation:

> Deliberation ... operates in matters that hold good as a general rule, but whose outcome is unpredictable.... When great issues are at stake, we ... call in others to join us in our deliberations. We deliberate not about ends but about means to attain ends: no physician deliberates whether he should cure ... we take the end for granted, and then consider in which manner and by what means it can be realized. (*Nic. Ethnics*, III, 1121a).

Practical action takes place where there is a 'plurality of agents'. This is the uncertain, haphazard arena of which Arendt (1958) speaks, and it is in this arena that professional, not technical practice operates. Professional practice is concerned with the intersubjective world of persons, not the world of objects, which is the arena for technical action. The entrepreneur, however, may also operate in the inter-subjective realm in which deliberation and choice are possible. What distinguishes professional practice from commercial? The distinction is in the nature of the guiding *eidos*. Professional practice is motivated by notions of 'the good'. It, therefore, has a moral component (note the importance of a professional 'ethic'). Hence, although a barrister may appear to be engaged in skill directed, outcome oriented behaviour (that is, winning a case) without regard for whether by doing so the cause of justice is truly served, in reality it is assumed that the adversary judicial system does serve the cause of justice. By engaging in that system the barrister who is acting professionally is furthering that ultimate interest. If, however, it begins to appear that our barris-ter is selecting cases to defend based upon the criteria of the ability of the client to pay large fees or the potential of the case to produce a large compensatory payment of which the barrister stands to gain a handsome percentage, then we would be justified in regarding the practice as more commercial than professional. It is interesting that within capitalism especially, the successful entrepreneur is regarded as promoting not only his/her own good but the good of the whole society. The transformation of commercial 'goods' (profit) into a moral 'good' is an interesting phenomenon.

With respect to this notion of the intersubjective world being the arena in which professionalism is practised, it is important to note that even though an action may take place in the realm of interpersonal interaction, that does not necessarily mean that it is 'grounded in intersubjectivity' (Habermas, 1971, p. 72). Intersubjectivity operates in the realm of 'I — Thou' (Buber, 1965). This is the interpersonal area of life. Strategic action, while having the appearance of intersubjectivity, actually objectifies persons. The relationships characteristic of strategic interaction are 'I — It' relationships. Objectified interaction patterns enable the making of analytical choices from within preference systems, rather than choice being dependent upon 'consensual norms [defining] reciprocal expectations' (Habermas, 1971, p. 92) between persons.

Although this kind of practical action parallels the deliberative, interactive, interpretative aspects often theoretically and ideally associated with such practices as law and medicine, it is not my purpose here to provide a basis for distinguishing between professional and non-professional occupations. I am concerned with providing a rational basis for the identification of professional action in whichever occupation it may occur. I am not arguing, for instance, that simply because doctors, teachers and social workers work with people rather than things, these are professional occupations. On the contrary, I am claiming that when these people work 'for', rather than 'with' their clients (treating the client as an object in the interaction), their work is characterized by craftsmanship, not professionalism. Furthermore, even in situations in which relationships of intersubjectivity rather than objectification prevail, if the decision-making which characterizes the interaction is strategic rather than practical (that is, consensus is based upon rules rather than upon reciprocal agreement), then the action is fundamentally technical rather than practical or professional.

When these stipulations are made it also becomes evident that, not only might the so-called professionals not always act professionally, but that so-called 'technical' workers might also act professionally. What is needed is not a designation for certain occupations, but an understanding of the nature of the work in which people are engaging.

When such action is analyzed more closely, it becomes evident that professional action, rather than being the superior form of human occupational action, suffers some significant limitations. These occur as a consequence of the nature of the structural environment of the practice and of the history of the occupation.

Beyond Professionalism

Aristotle's notions of *phronesis* and *praxis* assume a just or at least a neutral *polis* which offers no impediment to right action: one is free to act rightly if one wills to do so. This is not, however, always the case. The *polis*[3] can often constrain the actor in a number of ways, not least through processes of ideological distortion which make that which is a social construction appear natural. Thus there is a need for emancipatory praxis, that is, a form of praxis through which practitioners may become conscious of constraint upon just action and can free themselves and others from such constraint. We have considered in earlier chapters what this means in terms of the construction of the curriculum and teachers' curriculum practices. Let us now explore what, in general, this means for the nature of teachers' work.

The nature of this constraint can be identified if we return to what has been said in earlier chapters about the limitations upon practical action. It has been argued above that, in Aristotelian terms, professionalism is guided by the *eidos* of 'the good', and that this *eidos* is indicative of a practical cognitive interest. Habermas, however, has also identified the practical interest as the interest which guides the hermeneutic sciences. It is the agenda of the hermeneutic sciences to 'grasp interpretations of reality with regard to possible intersubjectivity of action-orienting mutual understanding' (1972, p. 195). What, we might ask, has a concern for mutual understanding to do with a concern for 'the good'? Gadamer (1979) provides us with a key to gaining this understanding through his philosophical investigations in the realm of hermeneutics.

An interest in 'the good' in Aristotle's schema is not simply a matter of cognitive curiosity, but rather a concern with right action. This concern is guided by the disposition of *phronesis* (practical judgment), and it is this disposition which Gadamer identifies as the basis of hermeneutic application; 'the task of Hermeneutics [is] to adapt the meaning of a text to the concrete situation to which it [is] speaking' (1979, p. 275). Hermeneutic understanding, as we have seen before, has a normative as well as a cognitive dimension (p. 277), which makes it subject to judgment (*phronesis*). This, in turn, implies that hermeneutic understanding has a moral dimension involving not merely correct interpretation, but right action. Gadamer provides the case of the person 'applying' the law as an example. The decision whether or not to apply the full rigour of the law will depend upon the magistrate's understanding and interpretation not only of the law but of the circumstances surrounding the particular case (p. 284). When Habermas speaks of 'action-orienting mutual understanding' with regard to the hermeneutic sciences, such action is not to be thought of as determined in the same way as technical action, but rather as guided by practical judgment in the same way as action is guided in the moral sphere.

In the analysis of professionalism given above, practical judgment was identified as the principal action-guiding disposition of practical action. It now becomes clear that professionalism is not simply present when persons act morally in pursuit of 'the good'. Rather, professionalism is a category of action involving hermeneutic understanding guided by judgment (*phronesis*) and knowledge. That is, professionalism is the characteristic of action which depends upon a 'reading' and interpretation of the situation in a way that calls for the exercising of practical rather than strategic decision-making.

Having identified professionalism with the hermeneutic endeavour, we need to return to the significance of the phrase 'mutual understanding'. Habermas brings together the factors of understanding and mutuality in a brief description of the historical-hermeneutic sciences in the appendix to *Knowledge and Human Interests*:

> Access to the facts is provided by the understanding of meaning, not observation.... Hermeneutic knowledge is always mediated through [the interpreter's] pre-understanding, which is derived from the interpreter's initial situation. The world of traditional meaning discloses itself to the interpreter only to the extent that his own world becomes clarified at the same time.... He comprehends the substantive content of tradition by applying tradition to himself and his situation.... The understanding of meaning is directed in its very structure toward the attainment of possible consensus among actors in the framework of a self understanding derived from tradition. (1972, pp. 309-10).

'Mutual understanding' is revealed as a shared interpretation of tradition. Gadamer, reviving the nineteenth century hermeneutic theory of the circular structure of understanding, portrays the circle as 'neither subjective nor objective, but [it] describes understanding as the interplay of the movement of tradition and the movement of the interpreter' (1979, p. 261). When we talk of the practitioner deciding upon action according to an interpretation of the situation, and when we reflect upon the action which practitioners take in such interactive situations, it becomes clear that there are traditions which suggest to the actor what is the appropriate action in a given situation. These are not rules of procedure. The traditions may never be articulated. But implicit in the practices of others engaged in similar action is a shared history and an understanding about what would constitute appropriate action.

It may be asked, however: What are these 'traditions' that are to be interpreted by the professional? Clearly, the traditions of any occupation are to be found in the body of knowledge, codes of ethics and shared 'wisdom' of that occupation. If we return to the Aristotelian notion of 'the good', it becomes possible to see that professionalism is not merely a matter of the professional person making individual judgments in the interests of the good of the client. Rather, professionalism consists in the understanding, interpretation and application of the shared traditions of the profession, for it is in such traditions that 'the good' is enshrined. As Gadamer notes:

> That which has been sanctioned by tradition and custom has an authority that is nameless, and our finite historical being is marked by the fact that always the authority of what has been transmitted ... has power over our attitudes and behaviour ... the validity of morals, for example is based on tradition. (1979, p. 249)

In the case of the professional educator, this analysis of what it means to enter into a form of 'action-orienting mutual understanding' implies that meaningful action follows from an interpretation and application of the traditions of the profession. In these traditions is enshrined the meaning of 'the good' for both students and teachers. It would follow from this that such traditions encapsulate 'the good' for the participants in any educational environment: that students should do neat work in their school books; that teachers need to establish their authority with a class early in their relationship together; that individual differences should be catered for in a class; etc. Such traditions are not articulated as the rules by which teachers must operate. They are (often unconsciously) shared understandings about what constitutes 'good' teaching practice.

For the professional practitioner, however, we must ask whether the established traditions of a professional *do* represent a distillation of 'the good'. To enter into professional practice is to accept that 'the good' of the client is to be served by these traditional practices. But whose interests do these traditions really serve? To ask such a question is to admit the possibility that the mutual understandings of those seeking to engage in meaningful and worthwhile practice may be less than complete. Furthermore, to acknowledge that there are perhaps other than the students' interests being served by the practices of the profession is to begin to realize that practical action has political as well as moral dimensions. Habermas identifies the task for those who would undertake such a critique of the traditions of a profession as being 'to determine when theoretical statements [traditions] grasp invariant regularities of social action as such and when they express ideologically frozen relations of dependence that can in principle be transformed' (Habermas, 1972, p. 310).

When we begin such a critique of educational practices, it becomes clear that unrecognized interests in domination may constitute many practices. For instance, does it really make for a more educationally meaningful experience if the teacher establishes strict discipline when she first meets her class for the year? Does such control provide for rich learning experiences or does it further other ends? Does individualized instruction provide the most meaningful educational experience possible, or is it possible that collaborative learning will be more meaningful? If the latter is the case, what interests do the rhetoric and practice of individualized instruction, which permeate educational practice so completely, serve?

Habermas argues that critique such as this flows, not from a practical interest in mutual understanding, but from an emancipatory interest. Emancipation is to be understood as both 'freedom from' the dogmatism of tradition that disguises an interest in domination in the cloak of an interest in client well-being, and a 'freedom to' in the guise of autonomy and responsibility. At one level, then, communicative action, is founded upon traditional practices which predispose the practitioner's actions in a way which circumscribes autonomy while at the same time relieving the actor of responsibility for those actions. For instance, the traditions of the teaching profession predispose the teacher towards authoritarianism, but at the same time relieve him of the responsibility of justifying his authoritarianism by legitimizing the actions through the sanctioning of professionalism. Moreover, such practices often constitute the client, in whose supposed interests the action is taken, as powerless in the face of the authority of traditional wisdom and practice. The way in which such practices constrain a teacher's work by disguising the lack of autonomy of both teacher and student in the cloak of 'good practice' reveals the subtlety of the distortion which is occurring. To be emancipated from such constraint, therefore, requires a different interest from simply a practical interest. This emancipatory interest will, in turn, imbue both the actor (the practising teacher) and the clients (the students) with autonomy and responsibility [*Müdigkeit*] (Habermas, 1972, p. 311). The *eidos* with which this interest is associated is still 'the good', but that 'good' is more clearly identified as consisting in a life-praxis (for both practitioner and client) free from domination.

It is possible, therefore, to discern another type of communicative action. Such action becomes possible when the practitioner moves beyond the realm of consensual norms to engage in emancipatory praxis.[4] Such action could be called 'radical professionalism', or, as I have proposed elsewhere, *practique* (Grundy, 1984).

Emancipatory praxis, having emancipation as its knowledge-constitutive interest, is not different in kind from Aristotelian praxis. It is a separate moment of human action, although not an inevitable moment.

> The emancipatory interest ... has a derivative status. It guarantees a connection between knowledge and an 'object domain' of practical life which comes into existence as a result of systematically distorted communications and thinly legitimated repression. The type of action ... corresponding to this object domain is, therefore, also derivative. (Habermas, 1972, p. 371).

Aristotle does not introduce us to emancipatory praxis, but he does hold that the highest form of moral virtue is possible only when practical judgment (*phronesis*) interacts with theoretical wisdom (*sophia*) (*Nic. Ethics*, V1, 1143a). This kind of wisdom embodies both knowledge (*episteme*) and intuitive reason (*nous*) (1141a). This parallels closely the connection mentioned by Habermas above between 'theoretical knowledge and the domain of practical life'.

Whereas practical action is realized through intersubjective understanding, emancipatory praxis is realized via the medium of critical self-reflection. Such a medium is to be found in a critical social science which 'is concerned with going beyond [the goal of nomological knowledge] to determine when theoretical statements grasp invariant regularities of social action as such and when they express ideologically frozen relations of dependence that can in principle be transformed' (Habermas, 1972, p. 310). This is the process of ideology critique which we have investigated in previous chapters.

Action following from such critique is informed by the transcendental *eidos* of 'the good' and by an immanent interest in emancipation. The emancipatory *eidos* is immanent because it is implicit in the very act of human speech (Habermas, 1970b, pp. 371–2) and hence in the fact of being human.

Emancipatory praxis operates at the level of social praxis, making enlightened insight possible, and at the level of political praxis 'which consciously aims at overthrowing the existing system of institutions' (Habermas, 1974, p. 2); that is, in the transformation of 'ideologically frozen relations of dependence'. Such action is characterized by a disposition which goes beyond professionalism. This is the disposition of *practique*.

A reconceptualization of the notion of professionalism, therefore, involves a revision of the concept of 'interests' as well as an analysis of human action. Professionalism is seen as being guided by a practical interest. This is an interest which suggests that 'the good' of the client is best served by prudent interpretation of professional tradition. *Practique*, on the other hand, employs the medium of critical reflection to 'get behind' the traditions to discover which traditions truly serve the cause of autonomy and responsibility and which (to borrow from Althusser, 1972, p. 265) present the real conditions of existence in an imaginary form.

Both practical and emancipatory practice involve practical judgment and hence *risk* on the part of the practitioner. Both forms come within the moral category, but it is clear that in each case that which is regarded as the relevant sphere of action is likely to differ. Professionalism seeks improvement in the lot of the client within the parameters and by the means sanctioned through the wisdom of professional tradition. The practitioner whose action is characterized by *practique* is prepared to trespass into areas not traditionally the concern of the profession, to seek improvement not only in the immediate lot of the individual client, but in the material conditions which circumscribe the client's (and his/her own) life.

Improving the Quality of Teachers' Work

The importance of ongoing professional development programmes for teachers is widely acknowledged within educational systems. The term 'professional development' usually implies some notion of 'growth'. Taylor (1980, p. 329), for instance, remarks: 'We know little at present about the types of experiences best calculated to result in professional growth ... experiences which promote growth for some may wither others.'

The agrarian metaphor suggests a teleological view of professional development. It may not be smooth and continuous, it may at times be advanced and at other times retarded, but, in general, given the right factors (if only we could identify them), the process of professional development occurs naturally, leading to some inevitable state of professional maturity. The concept of growth or development is not, however, adequate to describe the movement from a mode of work characterized by professionalism to radical professional practice. What is required is not transition but transformation of work practices.

If teachers are to move beyond a reliance upon the development and refinement of traditional practice into a mode of work which allows for the exercising of truly autonomous judgment, then certain conditions are necessary. Carr and Kemmis (1986, p. 9) identify aspects as being those relating to knowledge, control and action:

> First the attitudes and practices of teachers must become more firmly grounded in educational theory and research. Secondly, the professional autonomy of teachers must be extended.... Thirdly, the professional responsibilities of the teacher must be extended.

For such extension to occur, however, requires a radical restructuring of the way in which teachers regard their own professional growth. It can no longer be the case that teachers must be dependent upon the initiatives of central authorities or professional bodies to decide what constitutes 'good' professional practice. It is within the province of practitioners to take initiatives to control their own practice.

The practitioner engaged in purposive-rational action may be regarded as a mediator in the process of production. It is through the exercising of his/her skill that the desired educational outcomes are achieved. The practitioner engaged in practical action, on the other hand, appears to have a far greater degree of autonomy and be much more an initiator of action, but that initiative is, nevertheless, constrained by traditional practice. Traditions operate at the level of what Gramsci (1971, p. 419) would call 'common sense'. Since 'common-sense' ways of operating are no longer, if they ever were, subjected to critical scrutiny, it becomes questionable whether they any more serve the best interests of all participants in a learning situation. Practitioners working in this way, although reflective, conscientious and prudent, are, nevertheless, uncritical and see their work as being largely ahistorical.

Moving from being uncritical to critical, from being ahistorical to a subject who sees his/her work within an historical framework, requires, not growth, but a transformation of consciousness. This is the process which Freire (1972b, p. 128) has called 'conscientization': 'the necessary means by which men, through a true praxis, leave behind the status of historical subjects.' This is not a process of steady development, but a transformation which might best be called 'professionalization'. This does not imply a spontaneous transformation from constrained to liberated subject. Rather, it is a process of transformation in which knowledge and action are dialectically related through the mediation of critical reflection. This is a reflexive rather than a linear process, with the transformation displaying itself in increasing moments of emancipatory praxis rather than developmentally improved practice. The process of professionalization is a pedagogical process, not a developmental one.

Moreover, given the arguments in earlier chapters of this work, it would be no surprise that this investigation of the nature of teachers' work leads us back to action research. As I have claimed previously, action research does not automatically foster autonomous action. It can be employed as a technique which provides teachers with an efficient method of assessing and honing teaching skills. When used in this way it becomes a technique for improving the craftsmanship of teachers. Action research can also be used for professional development. It is a process which encourages reflection upon practice in order to understand that practice and make the learning experiences of the classroom more meaningful. Used in this way action research fosters interpretation and understanding, and promotes rational decision-making as the basis for classroom practice. Indeed, examinations of action research reports indicate that it is often utilized in this way by the professional development organizations within education systems. If action research is engaged in ways that are truly consistent with its epistemological foundations, however, it will become a process of critical pedagogy which will foster the sort of transformation of consciousness which is necessary for a process of professionalization.

This brings us back to the heading at the beginning of this section: 'improving the quality of teachers' work'. The exciting implication which action research has for teachers is that of opening up the possibility for practitioners to exercise a greater degree of autonomy and responsibility with regard to their own work practices, and to provide more authentic learning experiences for the students with whom they work. It is fitting in this regard that we take heed of the words of the late Lawrence Stenhouse (1975, pp. 142, 143), whose work with teachers provided for many a vision of the possibilities of autonomy and responsibility:

> ... curriculum research and development ought to belong to
> the teacher and ... there are prospects of making this good in

practice.... It is not enough that teachers' work should be studied: they need to study it themselves.

Notes

1   The gender-neutral term 'artisanship' is awkward here, so I have maintained a traditional form of expression.
2   As an example of this principle, consider Pericles' funeral oration in which he proudly made the claim: 'We do not say that a man who takes no interest in politics is a man who minds his own business; we say that he has no business here at all' (Thucydides, *The Peloponnesian War*, 11, 40).
3   I use the term *'polis'* here to refer to a social organization which may be a state or a smaller entity such as an occupational group.
4   I do not deal here with the emancipatory potential of unalienated labour. See Heller's objection to Habermas' separation of the concepts of labour and interaction and Habermas' response in Thompson and Held (1982).

Bibliography

ALTHUSSER, L. (1972) 'Ideology and ideological state apparatuses: Notes towards an investigation', in COSIN, B.R. (Ed.) *Education: Structure and Society,* Harmondsworth, Penguin.

ANYON, J. (1979) 'Ideology and United States history text books', *Harvard Educational Review,* 49, 3, pp. 361–86.

APPLE, M. (1979) *Ideology and Curriculum,* London, Routledge and Kegan Paul.

APPLE, M. (1980) 'Curricular form and the logic of technical control', in BARTON, L. *et al. Schooling Ideology and the Curriculum,* Barcombe, Falmer Press.

APPLE, M. (1982) *Cultural and Economic Reproduction in Education,* London, Routledge and Kegan Paul.

ARENDT, H. (1958) *The Human Condition,* Chicago, University of Chicago Press.

ARISTOTLE (1962) *Nicomachean Ethics,* Trans, M. Ostwald, Indianapolis, Bobbs-Merrill.

BARROW, R. (1984) *Giving Teaching Back to Teachers: A Critical Introduction to Curriculum Theory,* Brighton, Wheatsheaf.

BEE, B. (1980) 'The politics of literacy', in MACKIE, R. (Ed.) *Literacy and Revolution: The Pedagogy of Paulo Freire,* London, Pluto Press.

BERNSTEIN, R. (1972) *Praxis and Action,* London, Duckworth.

BERNSTEIN, R. (1979) *The Restructuring of Social and Political Theory,* London, Methuen.

BERNSTEIN, R. (1982) 'From hermeneutics to praxis', in *Review of Metaphysics,* 35, June, pp. 823–45.

BOOMER, G. (1981) 'Addressing the problem of elsewhereness: A case for action research in schools', Paper presented at the National Invitational Seminar on Action Research, Deakin University.

BOOMER, G. (Ed.) (1982) *Negotiating the Curriculum,* Sydney, Ashton Scholastics.

BOWLES, S. and GINTIS, H. (1976) *Schooling in Capitalist America,* New York, Basic Books.

BOWRA, C.M. (1973) *The Greek Experience,* London, Cardinal.

BROWN, L. *et al.* (1981) 'Action research: Notes on the national seminar',

Paper presented at the Eleventh Annual Meeting of the South Pacific Association of Teacher Educators, Adelaide.

BUBER, M. (1965) *Between Man and Man*, New York, Macmillan.

BUBER, M. (1965) *I and Thou*, 2nd ed., Trans. R.G. Smith, New York, Scribner.

CARR, W. and KEMMIS, S. (1986) *Becoming Critical: Knowing through Action Research*, 2nd ed., Barcombe, Falmer Press.

CHALMERS, A.F. (1976) *What Is This Thing Called Science?* St Lucia, University of Queensland Press.

COLLIER, J. (1945) 'United States Indian administration as a laboratory of ethnic relations', *Social Research*, 12, pp. 265–305.

CONNELL, R.W. *et al.* (1982) *Making the Difference: Schools, Families and Social Division*, Sydney, George Allen and Unwin.

COSGROVE, S. (1981) 'Using action research in classrooms and schools: A teacher's view', Paper presented at the Annual Meeting of the Australian Association for Research in Education, Adelaide.

COSGROVE, S. (1982) 'Negotiating mathematics', in BOOMER (Ed.) *Negotiating the Curriculum*, Sydney, Ashton Scholastics.

CURRICULUM DEVELOPMENT CENTRE (1980) 'Language and literacy', Statement issued by the Curriculum Development Centre's National Language Development Project, Canberra.

DEWEY, J. (1933) *How We Think*, New York, Heath.

ELLIOTT, J. (1983) 'Legitimation crisis and the growth of educational action research', Mimeo, Cambridge, Cambridge Institute of Education.

ELLIOTT, J. and ADELMAN, C. (1975) *The Language and Logic of Informal Teaching*, Ford Teaching Project Materials, Cambridge, Cambridge Institute of Education.

ELLIOTT, J. and HURLIN, T. (1975) *Self–Monitoring: Questioning Strategies*, Ford Teaching Project Materials, Cambridge, Cambridge Institute of Education.

ELLIOTT, J. and PARTINGTON, D. (1975) *Three Points of View in the Classroom*, Ford Teaching Project Materials, Cambridge, Cambridge Institute of Education.

FREIRE, P. (1972a) *Cultural Action for Freedom*, Harmondsworth, Penguin.

FREIRE, P. (1972b) *Pedagogy of the Oppressed*, Harmondsworth, Penguin.

GADAMER, H.G. (1977) *Philosophical Hermeneutics*, Trans. D. Linge, Berkeley, University of California Press.

GADAMER, H.G. (1979) *Truth and Method*, 2nd ed., London, Sheed and Ward.

GAGNÉ, R. (1967) 'Curriculum research and the promotion of learning', in TYLER, R., GAGNÉ, R. and SCRIVEN, M. *Perspectives of Curriculum Evaluation*, AERA Monograph 1, Chicago, Rand McNally.

GEUSS, R. (1981) *The Idea of a Critical Theory: Habermas and the Frankfurt School*, Cambridge, Cambridge University Press.

GIROUX, H. (1981) *Ideology, Culture and the Process of Schooling*, Barcombe, Falmer Press.

GRAMSCI, A. (1971) *Selections from the Prison Notebooks*, Ed. and trans. Q. Hoare and G. Smith, New York, International Publishers.

GREEN, B. (1986) 'Reading reproduction theory: On the ideology and education debate', *Discourse*, 6, 2, pp. 1–31.

GRUNDY, S. (1982) 'Three modes of action research', *Curriculum Perspectives*, 2, 3, pp. 23–34.

GRUNDY, S. (1984) *Beyond Professionalism: Action Research as Critical Pedagogy*, Unpublished PhD Thesis, Murdoch University.

GRUNDY, S. and KEMMIS, S. (1981) 'Social theory, group dynamics and action research', Paper presented at the Eleventh Annual Meeting of the South Pacific Association of Teacher Educators, Adelaide.

GRUNDY, S. and KEMMIS, S. (1982) 'Educational action research in Australia: The state of the art', in KEMMIS *et al.* (Eds) *The Action Research Reader*, Waurn Ponds, Deakin University Press.

HABERMAS, J. (1970a) 'On systematically distorted communication', *Inquiry*, 13, 5, pp. 205–18.

HABERMAS, J. (1970b) 'Towards a theory of communicative competence', *Inquiry*, 13, 6, pp. 360–75.

HABERMAS, J. (1971) *Towards a Rational Society*, London, Heinemann.

HABERMAS, J. (1972) *Knowledge and Human Interests*, 2nd ed., London, Heinemann.

HABERMAS, J. (1974) *Theory and Practice*, London, Heinemann.

HABERMAS, J. (1979) *Communication and the Evolution of Society*, Trans. T. McCarthy, London, Heinemann.

HALL, S. (1982) 'The rediscovery of ideology: Return of the repressed in media studies', in GUREVITCH, M. *et al.* (Eds) *Culture, Society and the Media*, London, Methuen.

HARRIS, I.B. (1986) 'Communicating the character of deliberation', *Journal of Curriculum Studies*, 18, 2, pp. 115–32.

HARRIS, K. (1982) *Teachers and Classes: A Marxist Analysis*, London, Routledge and Kegan Paul.

HEGARTY, E. (1977) 'The problem identification phase of curriculum deliberation: Use of the Nominal Group Technique', *Journal of Curriculum Studies*, 9, 1, pp. 31–41.

HIRST, P. and PETERS R.S. (1970) *The Logic of Education*, London, Routledge and Kegan Paul.

HUMANITIES CURRICULUM PROJECT (1970) *The Humanities Curriculum Project: An Introduction*, London, Heinemann.

HURLIN, T. (1975) *Questioning Strategies: A Self Analysis*, Ford Teaching Project Materials, Cambridge, Cambridge Institute of Education.

JOHNSON, R. (1979) 'Histories of culture/theories of ideology: Notes on an impasse', in BARRETT, M. *et al.* (Eds) *Ideology and Cultural Reproduction*, London, Croom Helm.

KEMMIS, S. (1980) 'Action research in retrospect and prospect', Paper presented at the annual meeting of the Australian Association for Research in Education, Sydney.

KEMMIS, S. and MCTAGGART, R. (1982) *The Action Research Planner*, 2nd ed., Waurn Ponds, Deakin University Press.

KITTO, H.D.F. (1951) *The Greeks*, Harmondsworth, Penguin.

LARRAIN, J. (1979) *The Concept of Ideology*, London, Hutchinson.

LAWTON, D. (1980) *The Politics of the School Curriculum*, London, Routledge and Kegan Paul.

LEWIN, K. (1946) 'Action research and minority problems', *Journal of Social*

Issues, 2, pp. 34–46; reprinted in *The Action Research Reader* (1982) Waurn Ponds, Deakin University Press.

LEWIN, K. (1952) 'Group decision and social change', in SWANSON, G. *et al.*, *Readings in Social Psychology*, New York, Henry Holt; reprinted in *The Action Research Reader* (1982) Waurn Ponds, Deakin University Press.

McCARTHY, T. (1978) *The Critical Theory of Jürgen Habermas*, Cambridge, Polity Press.

MACKIE, R. (Ed.) (1980) *Literacy and Revolution: The Pedagogy of Paulo Freire*, London, Pluto Press.

McLENNAN, G., MOLINA, V. and PETERS, R. (1978) 'Althusser's theory of ideology', in BIRMINGHAM CENTRE FOR CULTURAL STUDIES, *On Ideology*, London, Hutchinson.

McTAGGART, R. and SINGH, M. (1986) 'New directions in action research', *Curriculum Perspectives*, 6, 2, pp. 42–6.

MARSH, C. and STAFFORD, K. (1984) *Curriculum: Australian Practices and Issues*, Sydney, McGraw-Hill.

MAY, N. (1981) 'The teacher-as-researcher movement in Britain', Paper presented at the Annual Conference of the American Educational Research Association, Los Angeles, April.

MOUFFE, C. (Ed.) (1979) *Gramsci and Marxist Theory*, London, Routledge and Kegan Paul.

NEAGLEY, R.L. and EVANS, N.D. (1967) *Handbook for Effective Curriculum Development*, Englewood Cliffs, N.J., Prentice-Hall.

NOWELL-SMITH, P.H. (1954) *Ethics*, Harmondsworth, Penguin.

O'NEIL, M.J. (1981) 'Nominal Group Technique: An evaluation data collection process', *Evaluation Newsletter*, 5, 2, pp. 1–26.

ORPWOOD, G.W.F. (1985) 'The reflective deliberator: A case study of curriculum policy making', *Journal of Curriculum Studies*, 17, 3, pp. 293–304.

POLANYI, M. (1962) *Personal Knowledge: Towards a Post–Critical Philosophy*, London, Routledge and Kegan Paul.

RICOEUR, P. (1979) 'The model of the text: Meaningful action considered as a text', in RABINOW, P. (Ed.) *Interpretive Social Science: A Reader*, Berkeley, University of California Press.

ROBY, T.W. (1985) 'Habits impeding deliberation', *Journal of Curriculum Studies*, 17, 1, pp. 17–36.

ROWNTREE, D. (1982) *Educational Technology in Curriculum Development*, 2nd ed., London, Harper and Row.

RUDDUCK, J. (1975) *The Dissemination of Action Research Results: Conference Record 4*, Norwich, Centre for Applied Research in Education.

RUDDUCK, J. (1976) *The Dissemination of Action Research Results: Conference Record 2*, Norwich, Centre for Applied Research in Education.

RUDDUCK, J. and STENHOUSE, L. (1979) *A Study in the Dissemination of Action Research: Final Report*, Norwich, Centre for Applied Research in Education.

SCHMIDT, J. (1982) 'Jürgen Habermas and the difficulties of enlightenment', *Social Research*, 49, 1, pp. 181–208.

SCHWAB, J. (1969) 'The practical: A language for curriculum', *School Review*, November, pp. 1–23.

STENHOUSE, L. (1975) *An Introduction to Curriculum Research and Development*, London, Heinemann.

STENHOUSE, L. *et al.* (1982) *Teaching about Race Relations: Problems and Effects*, London, Routledge and Kegan Paul.

SUMNER, C. (1979) *Reading Ideologies: An Investigation into the Marxist Theory of Ideology and Law*, London, Academic Press.

TAYLOR, W. (1980) 'Professional development or personal development', in HOYLE, E. and MEGARRY, J. (Eds) *Professional Development of Teachers. World Yearbook of Education*, London, Kegan Page.

THOMPSON, J. and HELD, D. (Eds) (1982) *Habermas: Critical Debates*, London, Macmillan.

TURNEY, C. *et al.* (1986) *The Teachers' World of Work*, Sydney, Sydmac Academic Press.

TYLER, R. (1949) *Basic Principles of Curriculum and Construction*, Chicago, University of Chicago Press.

Index